INSIDE RIO

EXECUTIVE DIRECTOR
Suzanne Tise-Isoré
Styles and Design Collection

EDITORIAL COORDINATION
Sarah Rozelle

EDITORIAL ASSISTANT
Lucie Lurton

GRAPHIC DESIGN
Bernard Lagacé

STYLING AND PHOTOGRAPHER'S
ASSISTANTS AT INTERART PROD
Françoise Arnaud
Marcos Ribeiro

TRANSLATED FROM THE FRENCH BY
David Radzinowicz

PROOFREADING
Helen Woodhall

PRODUCTION
Corinne Trovarelli

COLOR SEPARATION
Les Artisans du Regard, Paris

IMAGE RETOUCHING
Fabio Victorio

PRINTED BY
Tien Wah Press, Singapore

Simultaneously published in French as
Rio, une invitation privée.

© Flammarion SA, Paris, 2012
English-language edition
© Flammarion SA, Paris, 2012

Flammarion SA
87, quai Panhard et Levassor
75647 Paris Cedex 13
editions.flammarion.com

Dépôt légal: 10/2012
12 13 14   3 2 1
ISBN: 978-2-08-020126-3

This book is printed on paper containing exclusively virgin fibres
made from wood sourced from sustainably managed forests.

INSIDE RIO

LENNY NIEMEYER

PHOTOGRAPHY BY **NICOLAS MARTIN FERREIRA**

TEXT BY **MAURILIA CASTELLO BRANCO**

Flammarion

Contents

FACING PAGE A view of the city of Rio de Janeiro seen from the twin hills of Dois Irmãos.

French Rio

The French presence in Rio de Janeiro dates back to the onset of colonization, when a Knight of the Order of Malta, Nicolas Durand de Villegagnon, attempted to establish what was to be "France Antarctique" at Cabo Frío. Villegagnon planned to turn the region into a military and naval bridgehead to the New World from which the French could fan out and control the Indies trade. Villegagnon's abortive adventure inspired a novel by Jean-Christophe Rufin entitled *Rouge Brésil*, which won the much-coveted Prix Goncourt in 2001. Like Villegagnon before him, the author adored Rio de Janeiro and Brazil, where he spent two years as cultural attaché.

The presence of the French in Rio since the Knight's epic exploit is evident in an impressive historical, literary, and especially architectural legacy dating from the turn of the twentieth-century *Belle Époque*.

At the end of the nineteenth century, Rio de Janeiro, in step with advances throughout the Western world, embraced values the French had adopted, such as democratization and the improvement of public spaces. The then capital of the Brazilian Republic thus embarked on a European-style policy of modernization.

Impressed by the work of Baron Haussmann in Paris, the mayor, Pereira Passos, had broad avenues carved through the city center. The implementation of this model also provided an opportunity to tackle chronic problems, such as the absence of a decent water supply and sewerage system.

This innovative urban fabric is encapsulated perfectly in the cosmopolitan layout of the Avenida Central, whose Parisian boulevard feel inaugurated the new era. This "little Paris," which opens out into the great square of Cinelândia, boasts a remarkable treasure of Rio's historical heritage, the City Theater. Established in 1909 and recently restored thanks to a partnership between the State of Rio de Janeiro and the private sector, it results from a fusion of two plans that was also a collaboration between two nations, for the architects who designed it, taking their inspiration from Opera of Paris, were Francisco de Oliveira Passos, son of the city's mayor, and Albert Guilbert, vice-president of the society of the Architects of France.

Intriguingly, one of the key city development projects in contemporary Rio also takes its cue from Haussmann's spirit of democratic urbanization: "pacifying police units" (UPP) form the spearhead of a vast effort to recover the soul of certain districts, to save them from violence, and to restore their civic values. Hence the Baron's template is perfectly adapted to present-day needs.

In literature, the French influence in giving a democratic face to the city is immortalized in the activity known as *flânerie*—or the art of strolling the streets to collect images of daily life. The great representative of this genre in Brazilian poetry is Paul Barreto (1881–1921), whose penname was João do Rio ("Rio John"), and who, in his masterpiece *A Rua* ("The Street"), gives free rein to his passion for France:

> *The street! What is the street? A Montmartre chansonnier has her sing:*
> *I am the street, a woman eternally green,*
> *No other livelihood was open to me*
> *Save to be the street and so, from time immemorial,*
> *Since this sorrowful world has been a world, that I have been.*

The street, whose destiny is to remain a public, civic space where the right to come and go is secure, where citizens can stroll or go about their business, through which men, women, children, and the old can move freely, this is a dream that we Brazilians share with all civilized countries.

Sérgio Cabral
GOVERNOR OF THE STATE OF RIO DE JANEIRO

FACING PAGE With its prevailing French influence, the Palácio Laranjeiras is regarded as an example of eclectic architecture. The façade is inspired by the Casino in Monte Carlo. A porch embellished with marble columns shelters the main entrance guarded by two life-size marble lions by Georges Gardet (see page 332).

Preface

Rio de Janeiro is a truly incredible city. Amazed by the combination—on a single picture postcard—of beach, mountain, and forest, we pass wide-eyed before the Botanical Gardens, the beachfront at Flamengo, the forest of Tijuca, the park of Boa Vista. And then there is the coastline, with the world-famous beach at Copacabana and its much-filmed promenade. But the charm of the "Marvelous City" cannot be reduced to even these scenic beauties.

As the former capital of the Portuguese Empire, and then of the Brazilian Republic, she also boasts countless jewels from centuries past. The convent of Santo Antônio dating to 1620, the Imperial Palace of 1743, and the great Arcos da Lapa—the vestiges of the Carioca Aqueduct erected in 1750—are just a handful of the abundant colonial edifices preserved for the delight of the eyes of Cariocas and of the many thousands of tourists who come to Rio every year. Strolling through the city center one admires the Municipal Theater, the Museum of Arts, the National Library, and a cultural center located in what used to be the head office of the Banco do Brasil. Then there are the Palácio da Cidade and the Palácio das Laranjeiras: the stately homes that are the workplaces of the mayor and the governor of Rio de Janeiro. Rio boasts more than forty churches and religious buildings scheduled on the registry of the National Historical and Artistic Heritage as architectural treasures of the city and symbols of Brazilian identity.

I would suggest, however, that beyond such natural, historical, and architectural treasures, our most valuable heritage is not material: it is the Carioca spirit and the bubbling culture of our city that make districts like Santa Teresa, the Ilha de Paquetá, Pedra de Guaratiba, Madureira, and Ipanema places full of grace and charm, both warmhearted and joyous. To preserve and develop Rio's culture and its quality of life are a mission and a commitment I have made my own ever since taking up my position as mayor of this city. Because to be mayor of the "Cidade Maravilhosa" is more than a privilege: it is an honor, but it is also an enormous responsibility.

Designed to revitalize the area around the harbor, the Porto Maravilha project is undoubtedly one of the most salient examples of this commitment. Awaited by Cariocas for years, the rehabilitation of the museums, cultural heritage, commercial zones, and housing of the port of Rio is one of the most glorious adventures ever undertaken by City Hall.

Yet it forms but one chapter in the story of the city's expansion, transformation, and rebirth. As the world looks on, we can only be proud to live, as it says in the song, in the "Marvelous City," the city of a thousand charms.

Eduardo Paes
MAYOR OF RIO DE JANEIRO

FACING PAGE Before the embassies transferred to Brasília, the Palácio da Cidade, built in a neo-Georgian style between 1947 and 1950, housed the Embassy of the United Kingdom and the residence of the ambassador. It was sold in 1974 to the City of Rio de Janeiro and today houses the City Hall (see page 346).

LENNY NIEMEYER'S RIO

A generous nature and a giving spirit have been the hallmarks of great hosts and hostesses since the first caveman visited his neighbor's cave and was welcomed warmly rather than hit over the head. Truman Capote is celebrated as a memorable party-giver, as well as a distinguished author, thanks, of course, to his legendary Black and White Ball. Jacqueline Kennedy, as she then was, is remembered as a peerless giver of White House dinner parties, overseeing each charming table arrangement and place setting. Marie-Hélène de Rothschild was known for the chic of her impromptu little Parisian suppers. And throughout society there are many others, lower in profile, each of whom has mastered the art of entertaining at home and making their guests feel totally at ease without the aid of fame and fortune.

Lenny Niemeyer is neither as legendary as the former (she still has plenty of years to achieve that) nor is she as unknown as the latter. And yet throughout many parts of Brazil, her mother country, her name is synonymous with great hostessing. Her home, overlooking the lagoon at the heart of Rio de Janeiro, is often the first port of call for personalities and VIPs from around the globe who would be hard-pressed to name the Brazilian president but know "Lenny" intimately on a first-name basis—whether they have met her yet or not.

Lenny. The name is also synonymous with the world's chicest swimwear and resort clothes. Brazilian of course. Is there another nation in the world which appreciates more the way that a simple piece of Lycra, cut and shaped with vision and sensitivity into a show-stopping bathing suit, can make a woman feel like a million dollars? Lenny certainly does and Brazilians, or anyone else who loves a beach for that matter, love Lenny.

Her personal style is the international uniform of stylish working women everywhere. A loose-cut white or off-white shirt, the sleeves rolled up. A pair of black or beige pants in a similarly lightweight fabric. Pearl studs in the ears. A little natural straw bag. A slimline gold watch with a plain leather strap. Simple leather sandals too. The hair pulled back in an uncomplicated chignon.

It is a uniform born of a deep understanding of how much can be pared down and how much discarded to leave the mind free to create. Her taste in home decor is equally unpretentious and defines "Carioca" style. Deep pale sofas, a large communal wooden dining table, and bowls filled to overflowing with freshly cut local flowers provide the setting for her traditional home-cooked Sunday lunches where anything up to fifty of Rio's who's who gather far from the spotlight to gossip and chat about what's what. As Lenny remembers it, there was very little "home entertaining" in Rio when she first arrived from São Paolo eighteen years ago after marrying into the Niemeyer family of which the world famous architect Oscar, creator of Brasília, is the head. Trained in architectural landscape gardening, she found herself sidestepping into the architecture of the body when her first batch of bikinis, designed and created in her home garage, became an overnight success.

Since then she has balanced building her company into a global concern with raising two children and inspiring the followers of fashion in her adopted city with her elegantly orchestrated swimwear shows, relied on each season to energize all who are fortunate enough to attend with their unique air of sophistication. ≋

Michael Roberts

ABOVE AND FACING PAGE The decor in Lenny Niemeyer's home testifies to the elegant simplicity of her couture creations and illustrates her fondness for the Carioca style: pale-colored settees, a large wooden table, and generous bunches of fresh flowers.

14

Lenny
Summer 2012
Croquis:
Cláudio BARREIRAS

16

FACING PAGE AND ABOVE Lenny Niemeyer draws
her inspiration from many sources: architecture,
art, and nature, as well as from her travels
all over the world.
RIGHT Lenny Niemeyer and her daughter, Isabel,
at the Canoas House that today forms part of
the Oscar Niemeyer Foundation (see page 272).
Isabel Niemeyer is wearing a piece from the
summer 2012 collection.

APARTMENTS

The City as Decor

"As this storm passed over the forests which surround the Corcovado,
the sound produced by the drops pattering on the countless multitude of leaves
was very remarkable, it could be heard at the distance of a quarter of a mile,
and was like the rushing of a great body of water. After the hotter days, it was
delicious to sit quietly in the garden and watch the evening pass into night."
Charles Darwin, *The Voyage of the Beagle*, 1839.

Rio de Janeiro is a dynamic city where nature, with her hills, forests, beaches, and lagoons, offers a steady supply of ready identifiable landmarks. One site particularly familiar to Cariocas is the Rodrigo de Freitas lagoon, which, between the sea and the mountains, caters for an abundance of sports and leisure activities. Rowers, joggers, water skiers, and rollerbladers, or simply walkers drinking in the views, make it a lively place. To choose to live here is to opt for a whole different lifestyle.

Standing on the banks of the lagoon, this apartment is in perfect synthesis with the environment. Everything is organic and mobile. The reflecting pool seems to project the living room into the lagoon and draw in the mountains, and the retractable roofs let in the vibrant glow of the metropolis, adding to the feeling of space and freedom. The astonishing staircase, its first steps anchored into the stone-built walls, curves into steps suspended in midair by a sinuous banister rail.

In these vast rooms, whose sophisticated interior has been designed with the occupants' quality of life in mind, comfort is synonymous with modernity. Painstakingly chosen with regard to the space, the furnishings answer all the demands of functionality. Everything has its place and its purpose, and nothing upsets the profound harmony with the landscape and natural surroundings. The wooden seats, armchairs, and tables cover the palette of natural brown tones, a palette which is enlivened by bright orange splashes of cushions and a red-painted front door that stands out boldly against the white walls and adds to the sense of movement. The absence of green in the interior is no shortcoming since it pours in from the forest rising over the mountains opposite and, closer by, from the palm trees surrounding the lagoon. The works of art lining the walls break up the predominantly straight lines and enhance the feeling of dynamism.

The apartment is evidently the creation of a gifted architect and a Carioca architect at that—one who learned early on to view his native city as a vast abode of human scale. Knowing where and how to live is an art and seldom can it have been expressed with the same confidence and simplicity that is seen here. ≈

FACING PAGE Giving onto the Rodrigo de Freitas lagoon, the duplex was designed as an open space in order to benefit from fabulous views to every side. In the background, the undulating mountains roll away to the horizon.

The astonishing staircase, its first steps anchored into the stone-built walls, curves into steps suspended in midair by a sinuous banister rail.

FACING PAGE AND ABOVE, LEFT A low, curved wall serves as a backdrop to a sculpture composed of dry branches inserted into blocks of concrete. The staircase begins in solid stone, but continues as suspended wooden steps, whose metal superstructure looks like a sculpture.

FACING PAGE AND ABOVE, RIGHT The interior decoration is contemporary in feel. The choice of white reflects the daylight and the bright colors, such as the main entrance door here. It also brings out the wide range of textured browns in the wooden chairs, armchairs, and tables.

Everything has its place and its purpose,
and nothing upsets the profound harmony with
the landscape and natural surroundings.

FACING PAGE The works of art displayed on the walls
deconstruct the straight lines, the empty spaces between
each piece creating a sensation of movement.
ABOVE AND FOLLOWING DOUBLE PAGE The lagoon extends the drawing
room to infinity. A retractable roof provides perfect insulation
from the elements. The divans facing the picture window
constitute an open invitation to enjoy the splendid panorama
of the Rodrigo de Freitas lagoon.

A Collector's Art

"A triumphal entry into what is an inland sea ringed by high mountains
and bristling with higgledy-piggledy rocks, enlivened by joyous beaches,
and sprouting with mysterious islands that, with the vivid shades of looming
greenery, blend with the dazzling sky and sea into an ecstasy of sunlight."
Georges Clémenceau, *Notes de voyages dans l'Amérique du Sud*, 1911.

Hardly has the door shut than one falls under the spell of this Ipanema apartment, not to mention the elegance and unpretentiousness of the mistress of the house. A vibrant sense of harmony emerges from the choice and arrangement of the works of art, each of which tells a chapter in the family's story.

The owner's father was a diplomat and she grew up outside Brazil; hers was a childhood full of literature, art, and music. When she reached twenty-one, she fulfilled her dream of moving to Rio de Janeiro. Now she can choose between gazing upon the splendor of the metropolis from her window or turning the other way to admire the contemporary art collection that adorns the walls of her spacious apartment.She began collecting when just fifteen with the help of her father, and today she shares her passion with her husband. The couple loves to meet artists and visit their studios, accompanying and sharing in their creative work. Their only criteria when choosing a new work to add to their collection is an acute eye and great sensitivity.

The couple commissioned the architectural firm Progetto to help them to create a place in keeping with their lifestyle. The success is plain for all to see: with plenty of space for future acquisitions, every room in the apartment is a delight. Brazilian artists—Tunga, Angelo Venosa, Ernesto Neto, Beatriz Millhazes, Cildo Meireles, Vik Muniz, and Adriana Varejão—rub shoulders with French figures such as Louise Bourgeois, Annette Messager, César, Arman, Tatiana Trouvé, and other internationally renowned names. Each work testifies to a special bond with the collector and seems to form part of her life. Everything is unique and exclusive: not just the artworks but also manner in which they are displayed.

Outside, the enchantment continues in the view from the terrace: the beaches of Ipanema and Leblon, the sea, the shimmering horizon, the heights of Dois Irmãos (the "Two Brothers"). The landscape gradually changes color during the course of the day, the surface of the sea reflects the sun's rays, and the odd cloud provides a touch of shade. The blue of the ocean and the sky melt into one. You can stand there for hours, just looking. In Rio, the light, the proximity of the sea, the riot of greens, the mountains, and especially the city's inhabitants convey a sense of energy one feels absolutely nowhere else. ≋

FACING PAGE A picture-postcard landscape:
the summits of the Dois Irmãos
and the Avenida Niemeyer frame
the spectacular beaches of Ipanema and Leblon.

The couple loves to meet artists and visit their studios,
accompanying and sharing in their creative work.

FACING PAGE, ABOVE, AND FOLLOWING DOUBLE PAGE Designed by the architectural firm
Progetto, the space houses a collection of modern and contemporary art,
including works by present-day Brazilian artists such as Beatriz Milhazes,
Ernesto Neto, and Adriana Varejão, which happily rub shoulders with
objects and sculptures amassed over the decades. The glass table in the
center of the room serves as a showcase for sculptures by Joaquim Tenreiro;
the figurines are representative of "Toy Art" that originated in Japan.

FACING PAGE The enfilade formed by the *Supreme Skates Decks* painted by Japanese artist Takashi Murakami leads to a portrait of Monica Vitti at the end of the corridor from Vik Muniz's series *Diamonds*.

ABOVE, TOP Annette Messager's *Untitled* photographs hung on nets, 1990s.

ABOVE, BOTTOM Detail of the skateboards by Murakami.

ABOVE AND FACING PAGE The art of collecting here joins force with entertaining style: a collection of mismatched antique chairs stands around the table. The colors of the room turn every meal into an unforgettable experience. On the rear wall, works by César and Arman.

Outside, the enchantment continues in the view
from the terrace: the beaches of Ipanema
and Leblon, the sea, the shimmering horizon,
the heights of Dois Irmãos.

FACING PAGE The blue of the ocean invades the space and is reflected
in the clear glass sculptures out on the terrace. Each work bears
witness to a personal bond with the collector.
ABOVE Works by Keith Haring and Bill Viola.

A Penthouse in Ipanema

Celebrated in countless *bossa novas*, the beach of Ipanema extends from the headland of the Arpoador, where people gather on summer evenings to admire the sunset, to the twin hills of Dois Irmãos and Avenida Niemeyer in front of the beach at Leblon. Opposite lie the islands of Cagarras and Comprida. Around the clock, sun-kissed passers-by make the strand and the beachfront a lively, invigorating place. This is the view from the magnificent apartment designed by Sérgio Bernardes and Lia Siqueira in the heart of the district.

The predominant white makes the apartment feel like a natural extension of the beach. It is a place that encapsulates that Rio way of life: the luminous blue of the sea and the sky seems to flow in, bathing every wall, every surface.

The large main living space is an open-plan all-in-one lounge, office, and dining room bathed in the dazzling Brazilian sun.

Light reflected through water pours through the ceiling in the dining area—in fact the ceiling is the glass bottom of a pool on the floor above! To the left, the office space has an inspiring view over the beachfront, the Arpoador, and other properties scattered about the landscape.

Designed by Lia Siqueira, the furniture takes its cue from the geometrical shadows that can be seen throughout the apartment. A hollowed-out tabletop thus coalesces into stylized leaves. The furnishings keep faith with the all-pervasive white—save for the dark hues of a soft leather armchair by Sergio Rodrigues. Sculptures of diverse materials—colored neon, brushed steel, wood, or bronze—reflect or emit light. Or they pose picturesquely, like the bronze fish by Brazilian artist Alfredo Ceschiatti on the edge of the terrace, which, seen against the ultramarine sea, seems to frolic in its element. The TV and games room boast "crab" and "caiman" chairs by the Campana brothers in quite a different register.On the middle wall of the dining room a photograph by Vic Muniz links the two levels; a staircase with a glazed banister rises to the upper floor where a salon decorated with *azulejos* panels leads to the terrace with the swimming pool.

The terrace shimmers with reflections on all sides, while the checkerboard pattern formed by the glass slabs on the bottom of the pool is stunningly effective. The roofed section of the terrace serves as an ideal venue for morning coffee, while the open-air area, furnished with seats and deckchairs, is screened off by panels of glass level with the sea to form an immense all-over composition in blue.

Such a place could be created only in Rio, where the landscape provides such a faithful reflection of the Carioca spirit, a mix of the essential elements of existence: sea, sun, light, and nature. ≋

FACING PAGE Here, everything is conceived to make the most of the light: the sun's rays, the shimmering waters, and the azure sky literally pour into the apartment's airy, bright rooms.

FOLLOWING DOUBLE PAGE The architects have turned this apartment into a natural prolongation of the sea that rolls into Ipanema beach. On the terrace, *O Passante* by Brazilian sculptor José Resende.

The predominant
white and beige color
scheme makes the
apartment feel like a
natural extension of
the beach.

RIGHT, FACING PAGE, AND FOLLOWING DOUBLE PAGE The simplicity
of forms and volumes leaves the interior space open
to the vast panorama. Designed by architect Lia Siqueira,
the top of the wooden table in the center of the room
is carved with a stylized pattern of leaves.

ABOVE AND FACING PAGE The light pouring through the glass-bottomed swimming pool on the terrace creates a pattern of broad squares on the marble floor in the lounge below.

Such a place could be created only in Rio, where
the landscape provides such a faithful reflection of
the Carioca spirit, a mix of the essential elements
of existence: sea, sun, light, and nature.

FACING PAGE The glazed guardrail opens the space up
to the endless blue of the sky and the ocean.
ABOVE The decked terrace and the chairs looking over
the sea are the perfect venue for family meals.

Between Sky and Sea

"Dazzling light floods the atmosphere
A light so colorful and so fluid that the objects it touches
The pink rocks
The white lighthouse towering above them
The semaphore signals seem to liquefy"
Blaise Cendrars, *Du monde entier au cœur du monde*, 1957.

Every district in Rio de Janeiro embodies a particular facet of the city. The beach of Ipanema symbolizes the fun and gaiety of the Cariocas. If Rio is known for a laid-back atmosphere and sensuality, it owes this reputation, without a shadow of a doubt, to Ipanema. The curiosity of the whole world was focused on this magical place by that much-hummed *bossa nova*, *The Girl from Ipanema* (*A Garota de Ipanema*), by Tom Jobim and Vinícius de Moraes, who lived near the beach at the time.

Located in one of the most attractive blocks on the beachfront along Avenida Vieira Souto, this apartment, designed by Thiago Bernardes, is the Brazilian home of a woman from Rio who now splits her time between here and London. Picture windows frame the beach and reflect the sky and ocean. Blue is the watchword, a color echoed a thousand times throughout the living space. Since nothing could be allowed to obstruct the eye-popping views over the sea and the strand dotted with colorfully attired Cariocas, translucent acrylic glider chairs hang next to the vast windows. Taking a seat, you can drink in one of the most applauded vistas in the world. For when the sun goes down in Ipanema people actually start clapping to express their appreciation.

The apartment is decorated with furniture, objects, and works of art discovered locally or brought back from all over the world. Pieces by much-vaunted Brazilian decorators, such as Joaquim Tenreiro and Sergio Rodrigues, stand cheek by jowl with Italian and Indonesian furniture purchased from international antique dealers. The sole selection criterion of these pieces being their beauty, the owner has forged a unique and elegant style in these vast but welcoming and relaxing rooms. Each object tells a story, while here and there a photograph evokes a memory of a shared experience with friends. As summertime lasts all year round here, people meet up and then continue the party out on the beach. So all Ipanema feels like the natural extension of the apartment. Inside one savors that heaven-sent balance between sophistication and relaxation. Nothing over the top; but everything is gorgeous. No superfluous frills: just everything the occupants need to enhance their life.

But that's Rio de Janeiro for you: a place where people from all four corners of the globe can feel at home. Just like in Jobim and Moraes's original song, in a "gentle to-and-fro on the way to the sea." A place that casts a spell over its visitors and offers them the gift of light. ≋

FACING PAGE The landscape laid out before the great picture windows forms an integral part of the decor of this apartment that looks down onto the famous beach of Ipanema. The Avenida Niemeyer and the hills of the Dois Irmãos can be seen in the background.

Inside one savors that heaven-sent balance between sophistication and relaxation. Nothing over the top; but everything is gorgeous. No superfluous frills: just what the occupants need to enhance their life.

ABOVE, LEFT The interior places a high value on comfort. Above the sofa, *Waterlilies after Claude Monet*, by the artist Vik Muniz.
ABOVE, RIGHT *Os Gêmeos* (detail) by Gustavo and Otavio Pandolpho.
FACING PAGE Adriana Varejão, *Swimming Pool*. Round-backed wooden chairs by Joaquim Tenreiro.
FOLLOWING DOUBLE PAGE The color scheme and understated elegance speak volumes as to the occupants' personality and lifestyle. Each painting and object tells a chapter in their life story. Painting by Daniel Senise.

Each object tells a story, while here and there a photograph evokes memories of a shared experience with friends.

FACING PAGE AND ABOVE, LEFT A mix of Brazilian rustic furniture and work by some of the best-known decorators in the country is the keynote throughout the apartment. A pair of leather and jacaranda chairs by Sergio Rodrigues.

ABOVE, RIGHT Photography is another collecting passion. Works by Neville d'Almeida and Mario Testino.

GARDENS

A Garden in Alto da Boa Vista by Burle Marx

Visual artist and landscape designer Roberto Burle Marx was born in São Paulo in 1909. The fourth child of Wilhelm Marx and Cecilia Burle, his father, of German origin, came from Stuttgart and had grown up in Trier, the birthplace of Karl Marx, who was a cousin of Burle's grandfather. His mother, of French origin, was a pianist and botanist, who transmitted these twin passions to her children. All four were brought up with a love of knowledge and culture. Roberto learned German and literature from his father, while his mother gave him the gift of music and his governess taught him how to recognize and grow seeds that they watched germinate in the family's kitchen garden.

It was the encounter between this upbringing and the exuberant flora of Brazil that molded the most famous landscape gardener of the twentieth century and the creator in 1937 of the first ecological park at Recife in the State de Pernambuco. The language Burle Marx employs is organic and evolutionary, and closely allied to avant-garde tendencies, such as abstract, concrete, and constructivist art. His use of ground-covering plants that create byways and alcoves among the local vegetation is often reminiscent of an abstract painting.

Growing into one of the most significant commissions of his career, this garden was planted in the district of Alto da Boa Vista at the request of someone who was already key to his early development. Burle Marx did not draw plans; the garden miraculously emerged from his daily observation of the landscape. A visionary mind, he would simply issue oral instructions to his assistants. The landscape designer saw himself as trying to conciliate three essential elements: the forest, the river that divides the property into two, and the house. And in this he succeeded in masterful fashion. The forest is brought to a halt by a border formed by an impeccable stretch of lawn that places the visitor at just the right distance to admire the natural exuberance beyond. The river that strikes through the property gradually broadens out until near the house it turns into a natural swimming hole. Judiciously laid out stone paths harbor other secrets, like this secluded basin surrounded by native *samambaia* ferns and other plant species. Steps hidden deep in the vegetation were built by the artist using stones found in situ, a subtle human intervention in a place where everything seems created by the hand of Nature.

This garden unites all the characteristics of the work of Burle Marx; wherever one looks, one sees his signature. ≋

FACING PAGE Regarded as one of architect and landscape designer Roberto Burle Marx's masterpieces, this garden in the Alto da Boa Vista district remains today much as he designed it.

The landscape designer saw himself as trying to conciliate three essential elements: the forest, the river that divides the property into two, and the house.

RIGHT AND FACING PAGE Burle Marx worked without plans, visiting the site daily and issuing instructions directly to his assistants in reaction to what he saw. His project integrates three components: the forest, the river running through the property, and the house with its intriguing roof and delicate French stained glass. The landscape designer created the outside steps with stones found on site; alcoves full of plants and pools hidden in the greenery resonate with the natural setting. The brook gently flows into a natural swimming pool opposite the house's terrace. Bromeliads, ferns, lilies, and philodendrons grow happily next to many other local species.

FACING PAGE AND ABOVE As the day proceeds, the changing light goes through every shade of green.

The Moreira Salles Cultural Center in Gávea

Standing in the quarter of Gávea and designed by the architect Olavo Redig de Campos, this notable building provides a brilliant illustration of the modernity and refinement of 1950s' Rio. The classic simplicity of its layout corresponds to an interior where every element blends with the furnishings to form a unique composition.

Presented with plans in several styles, the owner opted for a modernism inspired by the Brazilian colonial style, with openwork doors and windows, and blue and white *azulejos* lining the walls and floors. Extending over two storeys, the entrance boasts tall, smooth columns framing the door and contrasting with the plain pink of the wall and the harlequin pattern on the pink-and-white marble floor. The door leads through to a large atrium, where an openwork screen filters the light from the garden, creating a space where immaculate white is flecked with many shades of green and blue.

Composed in touches as if with a painter's brush, the gardens, over a plot of nearly two acres (8,000 square meters) bordered by the River Rainha, were laid out by Roberto Burle Marx and boast a collection of rare specimens of Brazilian flora, such as the *pau-mulato* and the *açaí*. In collaboration with the architect, Burle Marx also designed an adjacent garden that, viewed from the passageway to the side of the house, looks like an abstract painting awash with color and shadow.

With its generous panel of *azulejos*, the patio is another creation of Burle Marx and emphasizes the sinuous lines of the walls and a swimming pool that echoes the organic curves of the landscape. The building, that today houses a major cultural center devoted to the preservation of Rio's heritage, benefited greatly from the close association between architect and landscape designer. It is from this association that it derives its remarkable conceptual unity—its structure of rectilinear concrete blocks, rounded concrete elements lined with marble, and *azulejos* join water features that reflect the exuberant foliage and the colors of exotic trees from the Atlantic Forest and the flora of the Serra do Mar to testify to a synthesis between stylish modernity and regard for the environment. The absence of noise from the city can but contribute further to the quality of life.

It is fitting that the building should house a fine collection of pictures and photographs of Rio de Janeiro. Upon entering, the experiences and the values it promotes are immediately evident: those of a city dedicated to light and to the infinite nuances of green and blue provided by a verdant setting. ≈

FACING PAGE Built high in the Gávea district, this splendid house was designed by the architect Olavo Redig de Campos in the 1950s. Formerly the residence of Walter Moreira Salles, it shelters today one of Brazil's leading arts centers. In the neo-colonial style, it is surrounded by a garden designed by Roberto Burle Marx.

ABOVE Accessed solely through the living area, the garden to the side
of the house was designed by Roberto Burle Marx and Olavo Redig de
Campos to resemble an abstract painting.

FACING PAGE The entrance to the house redeploys elements from colonial
architecture, such as the typically nineteenth-century *mashrabiya*.

FOLLOWING DOUBLE PAGE AND PAGES 74–76 The sinuous forms of the poolhouse
melt into the natural environment; large panels of *azulejos*
by Roberto Burle Marx line the curving walls.

BEACH HOUSES

An Island Hideaway
in Angra dos Reis

"The sea is indigo, the sky blue, a parrot blue, with, in the morning and evening, cumulus clouds that scud, crumple, split, break up, and empty themselves like immense crackly pots which tumble over and smash to smithereens, spilling out their contents. An ooze of color spreading out before it vaporizes in the radiant atmosphere, a blaze of twilight, a blaze of dawn…"

Blaise Cendrars, *Brésil, des hommes sont venus…*, Fata Morgana, Saint-Clément, 1987.

Delightful! Located on one of the three hundred plus islands in the Bay of Angra dos Reis, known as Rio de Janeiro's "Green Coast," this enchanting residence sprawls delicately over a sizable plot of land. The rooms, chalets, and verandas, decorated in Provence style, all light and rustic simplicity, afford an interesting counterpoint to the marine beauty of the site. The owners, a couple and their children, are constantly surrounded by friends who love to come and enjoy this little corner of paradise where the greenery runs down to the boundless ocean and the fine white sand is licked by crystal-clear waters.

Set among the luxuriant trees, plants, birds, and the flat, rolled lawn, the garden plays host to a major piece of sculpture by José Bechara entitled *Ok, Ok, Let's Talk*, comprised of an array of rectangular tables creating a geometrical pattern. The level surface of the tables is interrupted by two chairs that protrude from small openings—like the anti-corrosion material in which the sculpture is made, chilly but given a velvety feel by the patina—imparting a sense of dynamism to the landscape and setting up a dialog with the sunlight and abundant greenery. The whole ensemble links the mineral, vegetable, and animal kingdoms.

The beauty of the location, the welcoming atmosphere and the open-hearted hospitality of the hosts fill the eyes, the mind, and the palate—hence our heading: *Delightful!* ≋

FACING PAGE Nicknamed the "Green Coast," the region of Angra dos Reis combines all the splendor of the sea with the luxuriant vegetation of the Serra da Bocaina. Its islands are a nature lover's paradise.

The whole ensemble links the mineral, vegetable, and animal kingdoms.

FACING PAGE Installation by artist José Bechara.
ABOVE AND PAGE 82 The Atlantic Forest is the natural habitat of a vast variety of plants, as well as of birds and mammals—such as marmosets and other monkeys, toucans, parrots, and the thrushes known as *sabiás*.
PAGE 83 The rooms are unpretentious and welcoming. The Provence-influenced decor is perfectly in keeping with the maritime beauty of the location.

The beauty of the
location, the welcoming
atmosphere, and
the open-hearted
hospitality of the hosts
fill the eyes and the
mind, and please
the palate.

RIGHT AND FACING PAGE The owners of this magical site,
whose magnificent natural location is a haven of beauty,
combine *savoir-vivre* with a talent for entertaining.

The French Touch:
The Insólito Hotel in Búzios

"Unusual" (Insólito): such is the name of this unique hotel established in one of the most beautiful quarters in Búzios, the beach of Ferradura. Two hours from Rio de Janeiro, this seaside resort flanked by gorgeous beaches occupies a wonderful site on a spit of land.

"Unusual" the hotel is first and foremost by its story—for it is the brainchild of a Franco-Belgian couple who fell in love with the place and, convinced of its historic and cultural potential, upped sticks and moved here. As soon as they arrived in Brazil, they felt at home, and very soon they had the burning desire to share their *coup de foudre* with others. Why not create something truly unique: a place where Brazil and France—two cultures that have been so close for so long—might meet? As a lawyer, Emmanuelle Meeus de Clermont Tonnerre undertakes this project and invites architect Luiz Fernando Grabowsky to reconfigure the architectural spaces already intelligently laid out by his predecessor Otávio Raja Gabaglia. Their desire was to walk the tightrope between comfort, culture, green values, and social imperatives, offering a socially acceptable yet exclusive service in collaboration with national artists and creatives.

In their work they were guided by two dominant principles: the hotel should both have character and be authentic. Hence the choice of a boutique hotel—a concept that remains relevant in an age when proprietors want to treat guests as individuals. Each room is thus devoted to a theme illustrating the culture, art, or design style of Brazil, transforming the art of running a hotel into a tribute to the country in which it stands. The hotel amounts to a kind of open museum, its rooms adorned with unique objects that evoke the music, photography, literature, art, nature, history, and design of Brazil, as well as the African influence on its culture.

In addition to the vista, the couple was won over by the abundance and diversity of local materials; woods with sonorous and exotic names such as *peroba*, *pequi*, jacaranda, *pau-brasil* (the "ember wood" or "brazilwood"), offered a vast range of textures for reconfiguring the decor made by the owner. Unearthing the individual pieces of furniture amounted to a veritable treasure hunt. Form and intrinsic beauty were the overriding criteria. Pieces by Sergio Rodrigues, Joaquim Tenreiro, Zanini de Caldas, Jorge Zalszupin, Ethel Carmona, and Juliana Llussa were among the prizes, but works by many others also fulfilled the owners' desires.

The instructions given to Anouck Barcat, the landscape designer called in to reshape the gardens, were to create a variety of environments and to lay out each space individually, with the accent, as always, on local materials and regional flora.

Hotel Insólito is a work in progress, one constantly being reinvented in the light of an aesthetic and sensitive concept that gives prominence to beautiful things which Brazilians themselves—used to seeing them every day—may sometimes forget. ≈

FACING PAGE Less than two hours from Rio, the seaside resort of Búzios charms by its glorious light and its relaxed but sophisticated denizens.

ABOVE AND FACING PAGE The Insólito has everything visitors could wish for:
lush vegetation and endless nuances of blue, combined with the owners'
impeccable taste that has made an inimitable mark on rooms adorned
with creations by international designers from the 1950s and '60s.

FACING PAGE AND ABOVE The original project by the environmentally aware architect Octávio Raja Gabaglia, a long-time resident of Búzios, was renovated by Luis Fernando Grabowsky. Green values here go hand in hand with social and cultural commitment.

PRECEDING DOUBLE PAGE, FACING PAGE, AND ABOVE Acquired over time by the owner, the collection of furniture provides a mini-museum of great Brazilian design by figures like José Zanine Caldas, Sergio Rodrigues, and Joaquim Tenreiro. Passionate about the style of that era, she is constantly on the lookout for new wonders—to the delight of her many guests.

A House on the "Green Coast"

Angra dos Reis is a historic municipality located on the "Green Coast" of Rio de Janeiro State. Its name (meaning "Bay of Kings") reflects the fact that a Portuguese squadron sailed into the Bay of Ilha Grande in 1502, on January 6, the feast day of the Adoration of the Kings. Nestling between the sea and the green vastness of the Atlantic forest visible from the beach and extending to the mountains of the Serra do Mar, it includes in its territory an astonishingly beautiful scattering of some 365 islands.

Built on the continent, the present house possesses special significance for its owners. It was chosen for the couple's son, who left them when only twenty-nine but whose memory is ever-present. He had always wanted somewhere to live on the Green Coast and this happened to be the first property they spotted, though it was only purchased a year later. Full of the memory of joyous moments spent *en famille*, the house exudes an energy all of its own. It is the brainchild of Cadas Abranches, an architect who understood exactly how the family likes to spend their time and who had already designed an apartment for them in Rio de Janeiro. Crossing the threshold, the atmosphere of relaxation is almost palpable.

With ample space for friends, the house is the setting for unforgettable moments throughout the day. These start even before morning coffee with a dive from the jetty, followed closely by the incomparable luxury of choosing the day's meal from the freshly caught fish brought in by boat. In Angra, the sea is never chilly. Surrounded by trees and exuberant plant life, the bay is strewn with a tight skein of islands, the best known being Ilha Grande, just ten minutes away by boat. After several hours spent in the ocean, a dip in the heated swimming pool while lunch is being prepared relaxes the limbs. A catnap, then a game of tennis or a little waterskiing continues a day of unalloyed delight.

Evening falls without fanfare, heralding the ideal time for a sauna. Indeed time is the house's most faithful ally; here, there is time for everything, even time just to simply drink in the surrounding beauty. Contemplation is interrupted only by the delicious smell of a pizza baked in a peel oven. Conversation lasts long into the night beneath the star-studded sky seemingly brighter than even the city lights. When sleep eventually beckons, it is against the backdrop of the sound of the water lapping on stones around the house's terrace. ≋

FACING PAGE AND FOLLOWING DOUBLE PAGE What could be more relaxing than spending a sun-drenched day gazing out over the ocean? This is the delightful prospect offered by the house at Angra dos Reis. Silence reigns as we contemplate the scene.

Unforgettable moments start even before morning coffee with a dive from the jetty, followed closely by the incomparable luxury of choosing the day's meal from the freshly caught fish brought in by boat.

PRECEDING DOUBLE PAGE The garden plays host to exotic plants such as the "jade flower," native to the Philippines and acclimatized to Brazil by Roberto Burle Marx.
FACING PAGE Built on several levels, the house offers various views over the sea. A retractable roof makes it possible to adjust the light and make the most of the breeze off the sea.

ABOVE Boats draw up at the private quayside to present the morning's catch.
FOLLOWING DOUBLE PAGE The keywords are harmony and simplicity—supreme luxuries.

Here, there is time for everything, even time just to simply drink in the beauty.

ABOVE AND FACING PAGE The most beautiful decoration for a dining table is nature's bounty. On the menu: tropical fruit, fish, seafood, and vegetables, all from the surrounding region. The tropical flowers were picked in the garden.

FAZENDAS

The Fazenda Santarém
and the Itajoana Stud Farm

At the edge of the old Estrada Real ("royal way"), which in the eighteenth century was the main route for gold and diamonds extracted from the Minas Gerais on their way to the port of Rio de Janeiro to be shipped to Portugal, lies the Fazenda Santarém. The main building of the *fazenda* was built more than 150 years ago, for José Mariano—heir to the Barroso Pereira family, important landowners in the Médio Paraíba region—and his wife Isabel Leopoldina.

This single-storey colonial house stands proud among the lush vegetation that surrounds it. The frontage is pierced at regular intervals with sash windows with moldings highlighted in green and colored-glass transoms. A raised stone entryway leads to the front door that opens into a large salon where visitors are greeted by portraits of bygone owners. On the right of the drawing room is the living room, whose two-tone floor in a star pattern is repeated on the timbered ceiling. Next is the large dining room where the enormous table in *peroba* wood can seat some twenty people. The family spends most of its time in the smaller, more intimate living room and the games room with its central fireplace.

In the course of more than two centuries, the *fazenda* has only rarely changed hands. The Barroso Pereiras were related by marriage to the Wernecks, another of the great landowning families in the region. It was only in the twentieth century, at the beginning of the 1980s, that Déa Werneck sold the estate to Olavo Monteiro de Carvalho, the initiator of the first restoration and modernization project.

Alterations included linking the formerly self-contained kitchen to the body of house by installing a wide corridor, the windows of which open onto a garden at the side where a swimming pool has been dug into the lawn. Along the new corridor closets and a pantry were installed, providing a place for the local sugar-cane brandy to quietly age in great oak barrels. White and garnet-red terra-cotta tiles cover the floor and walls with the same rosette motif. Once installed, Olavo Monteiro de Carvalho was able to put into action his plans for the Mangalarga Marchador, a Brazilian breed of horse whose history goes back more than 180 years. He set up a stud farm, the Haras Itajoana, devoted to breeding these horses in the traditional manner.

As the Paraíba Valley has been gradually repopulated, the region is coming out of its torpor and employment is on the up. In 1997, Olavo Monteiro de Carvalho founded the Instituto Marquês de Salamanca, an organization promoting local community development. Opening a crèche, he also created a local school, the Marquês de Salamanca. This partnership with the municipality set in motion a whole series of enterprises, such as the establishment of training workshops and the opening of medical and dental surgeries. In addition, the introduction of public transport has greatly encouraged workers to settle in the area. ≋

FACING PAGE The main entrance to the estate. The terraces along the side of the drive are still used to dry coffee. Built in the mid-nineteenth century, the seat of the *fazenda* stands at the end of the avenue surrounded by the natural beauty of the forest.
FOLLOWING DOUBLE PAGE In the great room visitors are greeted by portraits of previous owners.

FACING PAGE Warm and welcoming, the games room with its
fireplace is where the family likes to congregate and relax.
ABOVE AND FOLLOWING DOUBLE PAGE The *fazenda* is the site of a stud farm,
the Haras Itajoana, nationally recognized for the Mangalarga
Marchador, a traditional Brazilian breed known for its agility,
elegance, and excellent temperament for more than 180 years.

ABOVE, TOP The dining room is unpretentious and hospitable. The restoration carried out in the 1980s respects the features of the original construction; the corniced ceilings and the doors with transoms have been conserved throughout.
ABOVE, BOTTOM A typical *fazenda* kitchen. This part of the domain has been modernized and is entirely lined in tiles—including the huge wood-burning oven.
FACING PAGE The long corridor connects the kitchen to the main building and includes a pantry and linen room. Local brandy ages in wooden barrels.

The Fazenda Chacrinha

Valença, an historic city in Rio de Janeiro State, prospered in the nineteenth century as one of largest centers of coffee production. The site of numerous plantations, it was the stronghold of the coffee barons—the rural aristocracy that for an entire century bankrolled the economy and nobility of Brazil.

The entrance to the property is proclaimed by a cast-iron gate and swelling columns topped with lamps. Once over the stone bridge with its iron railing, there are various secondary constructions, including guests' quarters, a still, and, farther on, the stables. The cube-like main range emerges from among the flowerbeds, the house peering out from behind hundreds of fruit trees, among them mango and *jaboticabas*. Juçara palm trees, today an endangered species, stand next to hundred-year-old imperial palms, which, in the nineteenth century, informed travelers that the residence provided lodging. The domain's forest is jealously preserved and rich in fauna, birds and woodland animals.

The estate stands on raised ground—the external galleries and the main door flanked by period carriage lamps provide an imposing first impression. It is the side of the building that gives on the valley, however, which reveals its true magnificence and originality. The symmetrical windows—curved on the upper storey, but with straight lintels on the ground floor—are characteristic of the neo-classical rural style favored by coffee planters in the golden age of the Paraíba valley *fazendas*. Complete with a granite fountain, the entrance to the façade of the side wing leads to the great hall with its vast wooden staircase. The floor is laid entirely in Riga pine, some of the boards measuring over thirty feet (ten meters). The galleries and service buildings are paved in hydraulic brick decorated with a fleur-de-lis pattern in shades of green and guava pink. The interior boasts an important collection of eighteenth- and nineteenth-century Brazilian furniture that blends perfectly with examples of contemporary sculpture and painting the owners have collected over the years. The still has been recently restored, and now, as a result of painstaking attention to the alcohol content during the distillation phase and the oak-ageing process, produces an amber-hued brandy suitably christened "Chacrinha de Ouro."

Today, the estate is primarily a place where the family—which, among many other interests, devotes its time to breeding Brazilian Mangalarga Marchador racehorses—comes to relax. ≋

FACING PAGE The entrance door on the side front with its semicircular skylight leads into a large patio set with a stone fountain dating to 1850.
FOLLOWING DOUBLE PAGE The house makes its appearance behind flowerbeds and stands of fruit trees and palms.

FACING PAGE AND ABOVE, TOP The great covered veranda across the main front is notable for being floored with two shades of cement paving and for the contrast between the nineteenth-century architecture and the metal sculptures by the artist Amilcar de Castro.

ABOVE, BOTTOM Today, the estate is primarily a place of leisure dedicated to the breeding of the Brazilian Mangalarga Marchador.

ABOVE AND FACING PAGE The living room displays doors with beading in the colors of the national flag and is the ideal place to illustrate various periods in Brazilian art, from local landscapes by the academic painter Batista de Costa to the explosive colors on canvases by Beatriz Milhazes.

The interior boasts an important collection
of eighteenth- and nineteenth-century Brazilian
furniture that blends perfectly with examples
of contemporary sculpture and painting
the owners have collected over the years.

ABOVE AND FACING PAGE The domain houses an important collection
of eighteenth- and nineteenth-century furniture: coffee tables,
chairs, consoles, and roll-top desks. The splendid Dom José-style
Portuguese bedhead dates from the second half of the
nineteenth century. The interior doors are fitted with Baccarat
mille-fleurs handles in crystal glass.

The São Fernando Fazenda

Only three miles by car from the little village of Massambará in the district of Vassouras stands the Fazenda São Fernando. The town of Vassouras was the cradle of the great coffee plantations that constituted the bedrock of the Brazilian empire's economy throughout the nineteenth century. Brazil's most important export, "green gold" gave rise to a powerful rural aristocracy that built huge estates to house the coffee barons' families.

The Fazenda São Fernando conjures up this golden age. Built on a hillock, the family's seat had a panoramic view of everything that happened on the property. This *fazenda* differs from its cousins in the region as it is divided into two low-lying main buildings, constructed at different periods and only later connected by a passageway. The neoclassical influence is as visible on the façades as in the interior.

Erected at the beginning of the nineteenth century, the first building forfeited its role as the family home when the second, built half a century later, became the *fazenda's* main residence. The entrance is marked by a stone precinct; on the right, as was the custom, stands the chapel. On the left, the great hall gives access to a dining room, kitchen, and other quarters of more recent construction. The building contains numerous pieces of Brazilian and Portuguese furniture from the eighteenth and nineteenth centuries, including medallion chairs, straw-padded sofas, and an exceptional, huge wooden trunk with a diamond pattern known as "*doce de leite*," because it is reminiscent of a type of milk-based confectionery concocted in every *fazenda*. The corridor is lined with a collection of sacred statuary, including an impressive life-size representation of St. Anne and two archangels who guard the entrance to the chapel. This part of the dwelling comprises a basement with stone walls that double up as foundations to the edifice. This unpretentious, rustic space houses a large games room where, in contrast to the old building, modern works by Brazilian sculptors and painters mix with period furniture.

One can still see the ruins of the famous "quadrilateral" that surrounded the coffee plantations, today transformed into vast lawns. To the right of this piece of land the remains of the stone foundations and divisions of the *senzala* (slave-house) can still be seen. Opposite stands the barn where the cane harvest was stored, together with the base for the sugar press. All these constructions are integrated into a landscape laid with lawn and planted with tropical flowers and shrubs.

Today the Fazenda São Fernando forms part of the São Fernando Institute, a non-governmental organization that in partnership with the government delivers educational services centered on agroecology and historical and cultural heritage management. The Institute's mission focuses primarily on the local economy and culture. Its excellent work in safeguarding the environment and culture can be seen in every detail of this truly remarkable place. ≋

FACING PAGE The estate of the Fazenda São Fernando is undoubtedly one of the most interesting survivors from the golden age of coffee plantations in the nineteenth century. Erected in separate periods, the buildings were later connected by a passageway. The restoration incorporates the older ruins and the massive stone foundations.

ABOVE AND FACING PAGE The entrance stairway and ornaments on the frontage present their magnificent stonework. Stone-built drains around the house improve rainwater run-off. The basement of the estate with its massive original masonry walls has been converted into a series of large halls.

132   INSIDE RIO

ABOVE, RIGHT, AND FACING PAGE The protection of the local
flora and fauna is one of the owner's chief priorities
and he has made the *fazenda* into an institute dedicated
to culture and the environment.

ABOVE Among the sturdy stone foundation walls and wooden beams in the basement stand works by Alfredo Volpi, Frans Krajcberg, Adriana Varejão, António Bandeira, and other contemporary Brazilian artists. The contrast between the rustic backdrop and the artworks make this relaxing environment one of the most attractive rooms in the house.

FACING PAGE The stone walls in the basement constitute the foundations of the building. Today it has been converted into a games room.

FACING PAGE AND ABOVE The ground floor is remarkable for its sober
and elegant eighteenth- and nineteenth-century furniture
and a truly exceptional collection of sacred statuary.

ABOVE AND FACING PAGE Local woods and nineteenth-century tiling decorate rooms throughout the *fazenda*. In the center of the library, *Torso*, a sculpture by Bruno Giorgi.

140   INSIDE RIO

SAVORS OF RIO

Tropical Savors
by Chef Karen Couto

"All around her, peaceable sounds, the scent of trees, little surprises among the creepers. The whole Garden is pounded by the promptly more precipitous moments of the afternoon. Whence came the half-dream that enfolded her? Like bees, or birds, buzzing. It was strange, too mellow, too big."
Clarice Lispector, in *Family Ties*, "Love", 1960.

Brazilian gastronomy is a melting pot of influences. The tropical savors and vibrant colors of its dishes and many cocktails based on sugarcane alcohol, the mix of smells, and the creativity of a cuisine that blends regional ingredients and imports from other cultures form an integral part of the enviable good life of Rio.

The art of chef Karen Couto relies on quality local produce with an added pinch of European traditional cuisine inspired by the unpretentious Mediterranean influences of French, Spanish, and Italian cooking. Rio cuisine is an amalgam of Portuguese, indigenous, and African elements. With the arrival of the first colonists, the meeting between European gastronomy and local foodstuffs spawned a rich and diversified cuisine. Manioc, fruit, peppers, and everything the hunt and the ocean can offer joined forces with olive oil, dried cod, stews, sweets, and confectionery.

Fish and seafood are omnipresent. Already in the eighteenth century Rio had a register of oystermen and fishmongers. A good meal is inconceivable without pumpkin with shrimps, grilled prawns, or fish of some kind. Although grilling over a wood-fire is not a local tradition, barbecues have become a favorite way to entertain friends. The totally authentic Carioca dish however, remains the fricassee made of egg, manioc flour and rice.

Fresh fruit is ubiquitous and of extraordinary variety; as juice or in cocktails like coconut punch or the famous *caipirinha* (*cachaça* liquor, lime, sugar, and crushed ice), in salads and in compotes, or simply served as it comes at the end of the meal, fruit is found in a vast range of flavors and colors: purple *açai*, crimson guava and watermelon, pale greenish lemons, and yellow *cajas* grace every table in Rio and in Brazil more widely. Coconut appears in any and every sweet concoction, from candies, sweets, and cakes to the celebrated egg-yolk dessert, the *quindim*. The peanut is omnipresent from aperitif to dessert where it appears in "rolls" or in solid bars dubbed *pé de moleque* ("boy's foot"). Condensed milk also stars in many recipes, the most eminently Brazilian being a chocolate sweet called a *brigadeiro* ("brigadier"). One final ingredient if you want to enjoy this foody samba to the full: take your time! *Bon appétit!* ≋

FACING PAGE Brazilian cuisine is a melting pot of influences. The *açai* typical of the north of the country has become a national specialty, as have condensed-milk flan and coconut preserve.

Fresh fruit is ubiquitous
and of extraordinary variety;
it can be found in a vast range
of flavors and colors.

FACING PAGE AND ABOVE An infinite variety of tropical fruits can
be turned into cocktails like *caipirinha*, traditionally mixed with
lime, but also with *caja*, pineapple, or star fruit. Prepared as
compotes, jellies, or as some other delicacy, and served with
fresh cheese, they are a perennial feature of every Rio table.

ABOVE, RIGHT, AND FACING PAGE A typical Carioca meal: pumpkin with prawn, fricassee with manioc flour, manioc fritters, cheese brochettes, and a gamut of peppers as delightful to the eyes as to the tastebuds.

Although grilling over a woodfire is not
a local tradition, barbecues have become
a favorite way to entertain friends.

ABOVE Specialties from the states of Espírito Santo
and Bahia; prawn or fish *moquecas* served in a coconut
shell are much appreciated by Cariocas.
FACING PAGE A true Gaucho tradition, grilling over a wood
fire has become popular throughout Brazil.

The meeting between
European gastronomy and
local traditions spawned
a rich and diversified cuisine.

ABOVE There's no getting away from the peanut! Salted
as an aperitif, or sweet in "rolls" and nougat.
FACING PAGE Accompanied by shortbread cookies or cheese rolls,
coffee is an essential component in entertaining.

COLONIAL HOUSES

A Colonial Mansion
in the Tijuca Forest

Brazilian style can be traced back to the colonial style of the Portuguese. Over time, however, climatic and other influences have lent it its quintessentially local flavor. Among the features characteristic of the nation's architecture are two- or four-pitched roofs covered with terra-cotta tiles, vast, high-ceilinged rooms to regulate the temperature, sash windows, and beaten earth walls derived from local construction techniques.

This late nineteenth-century house on the banks of the Carioca River in the traditional quarter of Cosme Velho is a fine example of the colonial style. Its most immediately striking characteristic is its perfect suitability to the surroundings. The garden teeming with the most luxuriant tropical flora and paths marked by rocks seem to emerge from the middle of the lawn that leads up to the entrance. With masonry steps and tall cast-iron columns, a veranda along the main front protects the centrally placed front door standing between great windows emphasized by broad wooden frames, which together provide a steady source of ventilation for the ground floor.

On the storey above, a terrace with a traditional wrought-iron grille leads the eye over the canopy of the nearby trees, while the top floor offers an uninterrupted vista of the mountains forming part of the Carioca range and beyond to the Corcovado: the natural plinth of that unmistakable symbol of the city, the statue of Christ Redeemer. Inside, the house's keynote is set by soaring ceilings and shades of ocher and mustard that contrast agreeably with the lush green outside. The wide range of furniture affords ample opportunity for comfort and relaxation. Braided straw medallion chairs, venerable pews, trunks, and eighteenth-century wardrobes rub shoulders with creations by contemporary Brazilian designers, all complementing the sumptuous two-tone parquet floor.

Outside, the landscape appears almost untouched by the hand of man: the paths through the tropical garden follow the lie of the land. The pruning knife and symmetry have no place in this garden. The bright colors and sculptural forms of palm trees, dragon trees, bromeliads, canna lilies, bananas, and orchids enliven the plantings. The garden is dotted about with stones, ponds, and springs that conserve the most natural appearance imaginable. A delicate bridge emerging from the luxuriant foliage affords a particularly delightful surprise. The dazzling colors attract all kinds of birds and insects, enhancing the life and beauty of the site. Among the flowers and palm fronds shimmers a swimming pool, whose soft, organic forms mirror those of the stones set around it. That such a landscape should nestle in the heart of a vast metropolis like Rio de Janeiro is just one of the extraordinary luxuries the city offers. ≋

FACING PAGE Its windows emphasized by broad wooden frames, the white-painted colonial house stands discreetly amid the exuberant vegetation, including rare palm species that can be admired from the balcony.
FOLLOWING DOUBLE PAGE An enchanting feature of the brightly colored tropical garden is the little bridge that emerges from the vegetation. The mountains in the distance form part of the Tijuca range.

TOP, LEFT Harmonizing perfectly with the natural site, the organic
forms of the swimming pool are based on those of the stones ringing it.
TOP, RIGHT The ocher and mustard shades on the walls and the furniture contrast
with the mass of greenery and bestow a firm sense of character on the house.
BOTTOM AND FACING PAGE The symmetrical façade ends in Ionic pilasters. Adorned
with motifs and rosettes, the floor of the porch is edged by curbs of broad
stone that prolong the steps leading up to the veranda.

Inside, the house's keynote
is set by soaring ceilings and
shades of ocher and mustard
that contrast agreeably
with the lush green outside.

FACING PAGE The two-tone floor endows the dining room with a graphic feel. Its towering ceilings and generous windows mean the room is flooded with light.
ABOVE All the rooms in the house are graced with nineteenth-century furniture. Medallion chairs in cane, Minas Gerais sideboards, and Regency settees with straw-filled seats integrate beautifully with modern pieces, like these leather and jacaranda wood armchairs by designer Sergio Rodrigues.

An Urban Oasis

Dense vegetation prevails the district of Itahangá: here, the majority of the jointly owned houses adopt an environmentally friendly agenda.

As an example of the city's new lifestyle, the house offers an interesting reconfiguration of Brazilian neocolonial style. The most immediately striking thing is its utter simplicity. Traditional in design, the ground floor affords a lounge and living rooms, while the floor above contains the bedrooms and other spaces reserved for the family. Occupying the center of its plot, the residence is surrounded by lawns, a swimming pool, and a privately owned wood purchased at the time of its construction. The gallery at the front that greets visitors provides a link between the interior, the swimming pool, and a garden teeming with tropical species.

The owner demolished the wall bordering the terrain, and the woodland is now separated from the house by a stone path that leads to the main entrance. The clearing has been turned into a terrace—a haven of leisure and relaxation with colorful hammocks hanging from the trees.

Laid out with careful regard to flow, the interior boasts a space that displays works by both Brazilian and foreign artists, as well as family souvenirs—those tiny things that seem part of us and of our way of life. The living room is thus imbued with memories. Here, light is of paramount importance: windows and glass doors let the daylight flood into all the rooms. The traditional white-painted walls are enlivened with dazzling *objets d'art* in every style and all amicably share a home in which the watchword is harmony. Adapting to the ebb and flow of life, it is a decor that has grown up over time, with the result that the history of the house bears the imprint of all its occupants.

Any alterations have to fit in with the owners' commitment to green values and to a certain quality of life: new developments include an organic kitchen garden that produces food for the family and zones for compost and recycling. The decor revels above all in natural materials—furniture and light fittings are all individually handcrafted from wood and various fibers. The sense of comfort and wellbeing that emanates from this building as it nestles among plants in every tone of green is tangible. Its note of refinement comes from the simplicity of both the home and its environment. ≋

FACING PAGE The house's principal entry seen through the trees in the private wood. The residence communes with nature through the vast picture windows along the façade.

ABOVE AND FACING PAGE A gallery runs practically round the
entire house, extending the garden into the zone around
the swimming pool, where the family likes to meet up.

166 INSIDE RIO

As an example of the city's
new lifestyle, the house offers
an interesting reconfiguration
of Brazilian neocolonial style.

FACING PAGE AND BOTTOM, LEFT Palm trees gaze down on the swimming pool
in front of the terrace. The private wood has been carefully preserved.
TOP In a natural clearing, brightly colored hammocks hang from
the trees, providing an opportunity to enjoy the natural setting.
BOTTOM, RIGHT On the vast lawn stand bronze sculptures by Bruno Giorgi
and Evandro Carneiro, the creator of this piece entitled *Rest*.

The traditional white-painted walls are enlivened with dazzling objets d'art in every style and all amicably share a home in which the watchword is harmony.

TOP A sculpture in Carrara marble by Bruno Giorgi.
BOTTOM, LEFT The miniature flags on this canvas by Alfredo Volpi provide an explosion of color at the entrance.
BOTTOM, RIGHT Painting from the series *Reels* by Iberê Camargo and a chaise longue by Le Corbusier.
FACING PAGE The wooden flooring and white walls of the ample airy rooms are an ideal backdrop to a collection of Brazilian art. At the rear, the series of studies of feet is by Candido Portinari.

Adapting to the ebb and flow of life,
it is a decor that has grown up over time,
with the result that the history of the house
bears the imprint of all its occupants.

ABOVE AND FACING PAGE On the first floor, the master bedroom is
dedicated to family souvenirs. The shells encrusted into the wall
contain various small treasures. Farther back, the door to the
cloakroom is adorned with glass plates depicting Brazilian birds.

A Showcase
for Contemporary Art

On one of the many hills of Rio de Janeiro, in the Santa Teresa quarter, stands the residence belonging to the industrialist Olavo Monteiro de Carvalho. Designed by architect Wladimir Alves de Souza in the Brazilian colonial style, the house, enjoying priceless views over one of the most beautiful panoramas in the entire city, puts comfort first.

The main entrance, flanked by imperial palms, is surrounded by an immense garden of tropical exuberance; visitors are greeted by a low stone precinct and an arched wooden door comprising six high-relief panels. In the vestibule a substantial canvas by a French artist, Louis-Aimable Crapelet, shows Outeiro da Glória at the beginning of the nineteenth century and much the same view can be savored today through the windows of the wintergarden adjoining the dining room. On the console below the painting, a visitors' book and some large Medici vases in Baccarat crystal offer a hint of sobriety to the interior.

Although the architecture is wholly colonial in style, modern and contemporary art also enjoys pride of place, tastefully chosen and wholeheartedly Brazilian. Styles, artists, and decorators from every age play a part in the composition. Two symmetrical doors leading to the lounge and dining room frame a delicate work in blue tones by one of Brazil's greatest painters, Alfredo Volpi. On the half-landing of the staircase rising to the mezzanine stands a wooden sculpture by Frans Krajsberg—a white-painted denizen of the forest who seems to pour over the wall like a wave. In the dining room an Aubusson tapestry shows a European landscape, while the painted chairs around the circular table, fine examples of Portuguese painted furniture, were made by the Espírito Santo Foundation in Portugal. Modern canvases by Emiliano Di Cavalcanti and Tomas Santa Rosa add a lively note to the understated calm of the whole in a color scheme echoed in the East India Company dishes aligned on the shelves.

The wintergarden leads out from the dining room, where furniture by Sergio Rodrigues and a round glass-and-granite table provide a wonderful foil to a splendid view of the city that takes in both the Sugar Loaf and Christ the Redeemer of Corcovado and the enchanted forest of Tijuca. At the back of the wintergarden, a side entrance gives access to a stone-laid patio on the lower floor.

The door to the right of the hall leads to a living room boasting works by Brazilian artists such as Cícero Dias, Djanira da Mota e Silva, Reynaldo da Fonseca, and Bruno Giorgi, judiciously arranged among European furnishings—a French flat-top desk, pieces of English cabinetmaking—and a monumental Coromandel screen framing the mantelpiece on which stands a traditional ormolu clock. Opposite, the sofas are accompanied by a pair of Barcelona chairs by Mies van der Rohe. To the rear, the wainscoted library abounds in rare books and artworks collected by the family over the years. The top of table in the center displays a collage by the artist Rosa Klabin, while the pictures dotted about bring a sense of lightness and contemporary Brazilian flair.

FACING PAGE A lawn planted with imperial palms comes to a halt in front of the porch protecting the entrance to the residence.

On from the lounge, the gallery is separated from an immense veranda by a picture window; the staircase leads to the great salon on the lower floor that opens onto the side entrance to the house. The lawn in front surrounds a swimming pool, and the garden plays host to bronze sculptures by Alfredo Ceschiatti.

The lounge turns the spotlight on Brazilian design, with furniture chiefly by Joaquim Tenreiro and an oval armchair by Ricardo Fasanello. Contrast is afforded by contemporary artists such as Ernesto Neto and Vic Muniz, photographs by Bern Stern and a series of views of Santa Teresa, including the Largo do Curvello and the Largo das Neves, all by local artists, including Iberê Camargo and Milton da Costa. It all gives the impression of going for a walk around Santa Teresa without ever having to leave the house.

The residence's gardens have been transformed into an inner-city sanctuary for the indigenous fauna: toucans, *maritacas*, and *sabias* fly by, breeding guinea-fowl saunter freely throughout the property—not to mention the marmosets and *agoutis*. To the side of the house, a triple waterfall tumbles into basins that are filled with carp and adorned with sculptures by Roberto Sá representing children playing with fish. As evening falls, the windows in the wintergarden afford a view of the lights coming on all over the city and the sky veering to a pinky orange. At six, the bells of nearby churches ring out as if to hail the illuminated Christ the Redeemer on the Corcovado hill opposite. This is a truly enchanted place. ≋

ABOVE AND FACING PAGE The side front looks over a swimming pool surrounded by an immense lawn. The balconies on the floors above offer panoramic views over the Tijuca forest, the Corcovado, and the statue of Christ the Redeemer, the symbol of the city. *The Silvery Fish*, a bronze sculpture by Roberto Sá, feels perfectly at home in the natural setting.

ABOVE The stone patio at the end of the wintergarden leads to the garden proper. In the distance is a glimpse of the Corcovado.

RIGHT The city of Rio de Janeiro as illustrated by Alfredo Volpi, one of Brazil's greatest painters.

FACING PAGE, TOP LEFT AND BOTTOM Inside the wintergarden, a pair of armchairs by Sergio Rodrigues.

FACING PAGE, TOP RIGHT Near the house, a succession of stone basins are used for breeding carp. Environmental safeguard is one of the priorities of the estate on which birds can be observed in their natural habitat.

It all gives the impression of going for a walk around Santa Teresa without ever having to leave the house.

FACING PAGE AND ABOVE The covered terrace in the main room boasts spectacular views. A sardonic touch is given by a selection of watercolors by caricaturists such as J. Carlos and Trinaz Fox on politics and football.

CONTEMPORARY ARCHITECTURE

Functionalism and Esthetics in the Forest of Petrópolis

Out in the forest of Petrópolis, an hour and a half from Rio, Jorge and Angelica Nobrega decided to build a country retreat to receive their family and friends. Designed by the architect Paulo Jacobsen, its plan was devised in three dimensions, with the overriding intention of integrating the architecture into nature to make the most of the local topography—which explains how some of the rooms have ended up nestled in hollows in the ground. Several low-lying independent buildings nestle into the landscape. Looking down a succession of porticoes, elements in concrete and slabs of plant material stand out discreetly against the landscape. To achieve a balance between architectonic function and innovative esthetics, the precise type of laminated wood required for the structure was only arrived at after a program of specialist research. The vertical struts frame the view and ensure the temperatures remain comfortable, while the ceiling is crisscrossed by horizontal blades.

Access to the house is gained via a paved path that leads to an overhang forming a porch. From this viewpoint there are dazzling vistas over the mountainside beyond. Out from the central range where the couple actually lives stand outbuildings housing the spa and the pool, a wing for the children, an indoor tennis court and, farther away, accommodation for staff. The principal dwelling aligns lounge and dining room, bathroom, kitchen, office, guest room, and beyond a terrace giving on the swimming pool. The guest rooms can be closed off by swiveling lathe panels. The basement features a garage, an office, a bathroom, a utility room, and the home cinema.

The splendid grand piano, the up-to-the-minute equipment, the sophisticated wine cellar, and the collection of artworks testify to the owners' passion for music, cinema, wine, and art. Compositions by José Bechara, Miguel Rio Branco, Nelson Leirner, and Daniel Senise stand nonchalantly throughout the house. The handpicked furniture and decorative objects were measured to the millimeter.

The children's house, where they enjoy a certain degree of independence, includes four bedrooms with en suite bathroom set around a lounge and a fitted kitchen. From the tennis court, one can see the wall that conceals the annexes—the kitchens, washhouse, storeroom, and pantry. The well-appointed kitchen is protected by a timber structure borne on slender metal columns.

Part of the construction is covered with vegetated roofing, ensuring greater comfort when temperatures rise or fall. The fireplace and interior gardens help control the temperature and add a touch of warmth in winter. Large glass panels and openwork screens let in the natural light. As light conditions change, so does the atmosphere in the house. In daytime, the porticoes create a dramatic contrast between light and shade; come nightfall, the lighting turns it into a haven of calm. ≋

FACING PAGE The structural balance between function and esthetics was attained only after much intensive research by the architect.
FOLLOWING DOUBLE PAGE Designed to fit in with the local topography and adapted to the uneven terrain on which parts of it are situated, this house in the forest of Petrópolis is superbly integrated into its natural surroundings.

ABOVE AND FACING PAGE The generously proportioned swimming
pool extends into the interior spa, giving unity to this zone of
the residence that is devoted to sport and relaxation.

PRECEDING DOUBLE PAGE, FACING PAGE, AND ABOVE The interior is laid out primarily in accordance with the family's joint passions of music, reading, good wine, and gastronomy; the openwork screens let the maximum amount of daylight possible into the vast living spaces. Chosen by the owners, the furniture and decor objects cohabit happily with works by contemporary talents such as José Bechara, Miguel Rio Branco, Nelson Leirner, and Daniel Senise.

To achieve a balance between architectonic function and innovative esthetics, the precise type of laminated wood required for the structure was only decided upon after a program of specialized research.

ABOVE AND FACING PAGE The immense picture windows open up the entire house to the magnificent surrounding scenery. The house is reached down a paved path leading to an overhanging structure that forms a glazed porch and offers a dazzling view over the mountainside.

A Unique House for a Unique Collection

"On the whole earth – and anyone having seen it once will agree with me—there is no more beautiful city, and it is unlikely that there exists one more unfathomable, more difficult to get to know. There seems no end to its mysteries." **Stefan Zweig**, *Brazil. Land of the Future,* 1942.

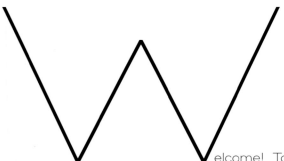

Welcome! To the south of Rio, in the light that splashes the landscape in typical Carioca colors, one lucky couple has built a large, bright house as a setting for their great shared passion: the vast collection of contemporary art they have amassed over the years.

The architect Gisele Taranto designed the residence to fit in with the lifestyle of collectors eager to live with their art on a daily basis. Since their other love is receiving guests, the house soon became a paragon of the art of entertaining in Rio. The presence of so many works of art hones the eye and sensibility of guests and visitors alike. For the owners, the idea of collecting without sharing their love of beautiful things would be unthinkable.

Among all the artistic languages represented, minimalism, with its geometrical forms, straight lines, simple contrasts, and relaxed esthetics, imposes its understated elegance. Standing next to examples of constructive art, abstract pieces dialog with more figurative works to create a visual symphony of color. Sculptures, paintings, drawings, wall drawings, videos, assemblages, collages, photographs, and objects: without ever losing sight of the main thrust of contemporary art, a host of signatures, origins, dates, and styles are welcomed into this collection.

The house's open, creative, and livable plan provides the perfect backdrop for a collection enhanced by the abstract style of the decor and the modernity of the furniture, objects, and lighting solutions. Exuberantly green, the garden invades the interior as if it to form a bridge between nature and culture.

Inside, photographs taken all over the world set off the beauty and chromatic richness of both the house and the collection it contains. As if on a pleasurable yet culturally enriching tour, visitors are encouraged to walk from room to room, drinking in the decor and admiring the artworks hanging on the walls or propped on tables and dressers. In this house dedicated entirely to beauty, contemporary art constitutes its very soul. ≋

FACING PAGE The tropical garden at the entrance was designed by Roberto Burle Marx and envelops the house in abundant greenery.

ABOVE Water flows over glazed ceramic sculptures
into a basin in the garden.
FACING PAGE The majestic main door in solid timber
towers over twenty feet tall.

PRECEDING DOUBLE PAGE The terraces surrounding the house
create a series of vast, welcoming spaces. The interior
volumes have been specially conceived to house the
prestigious collection of international contemporary art
acquired by the owners over the years.
ABOVE AND FACING PAGE The residence is in keeping with
the collectors' desire to live with their art every day.
As their other love is receiving guests, the house
is a temple for the art of entertaining.

206

ABOVE AND FACING PAGE The house's exposed metal armature casts geometrical shadows on the garden. Bromeliads, birds of paradise, porcelain roses, and other tropical flowers look like especially colorful sculptures.

FOLLOWING DOUBLE PAGE The house seen from the swimming pool.

The house's creative open plan
provides the perfect backdrop
for an art collection enhanced
by the abstract style of
the decor and the modernity
of the furniture, objects,
and lighting solutions.

FACING PAGE AND ABOVE Sculptures, paintings, drawings, assemblages,
collages, photographs, objets d'art, and furniture all from the house's
collection. The names, origins, dates, and styles are chosen with a
single criterion in mind: to exemplify contemporary art in all its forms.

An Architect's House
in the Tropical Rainforest

"There, the vegetation never rests and all year round the woods
and countryside are bedecked in gorgeous flowers. Untouched forests
as old as time outspread their grandeur virtually to the gates of the city,
forming a glorious contrast with the works of men."

Auguste de Saint-Hilaire, *Voyage dans les provinces de Rio de Janeiro et de Minas Gerais*, 1830.

Rio de Janeiro possesses more than its fair share of magical places. This house, for example, that stands beneath the symbolic Rio landmark of the Pedra de Gávea and is dedicated to leisure and the good life. Facing the beach of São Conrado, far from the madding crowd and sheltered by the great Atlantic Forest, it is in fact only five minutes from the one of the busiest downtown areas. In such a wonderful location, the birds and animals of the forest are never far away.

Designed as a home for his family by a keen young architect aged just thirty, it took five years to build and its designer had personally to put hand to trowel, directing the works and transporting materials. Consummately simple in plan, the house stands out with its large double-pitch roof and its *maçaranduba* frame (at the time timber from the Amazon Basin was still employed in building). The bamboo-clad ceiling was erected by local craftsmen, at home with the material but unaccustomed to working on such a scale. This cladding extends over the whole entrance, the veranda, and the lounge, which, in addition to natural light and all-year ventilation, possesses unusually high ceilings, making for generous volumes. Bay windows predominate in the living area: nothing obstructs the impregnable view over sea and forest.

The style and placement of the furniture are relatively informal, with the accent placed on family pastimes and entertaining, in true Carioca fashion. Works by renowned artists, often personal friends of the architect, like Vik Muniz, Nelson Felix, and Artur Lescher, stand next to objects brought back from journeys throughout Brazil and farther afield. The plan of the house has adapted with ease to changes in the family setup. Rooms have been knocked through or partitioned off, and now there's a music room, painting studio, and architecture bureau, as well as a sauna and a gym. Even the shape of the swimming pool was altered. Lastly, the floor was paved with granite flagstones that cover the outside zones of the living space and the entire interior, conferring a satisfying sense of unity.

In spite of all these transformations, the house has kept its soul of wood, bamboo, and glass, without forfeiting anything in terms of comfort and welcome. More than just a splendid piece of architecture, it is a haven of peace for the family and offers a perfect illustration of Carioca charm and flair. ≋

FACING PAGE Buried in the Atlantic Forest, and standing on the slope below the famous Pedra da Gávea and facing the beach of São Conrado, the house seems bathed in solitude, but it is in fact no more than five minutes from the hustle and bustle of the city. The nearby forest encourages close interaction between the local fauna and the human habitation.

Consummately simple in plan, the house
stands out with its large double-pitch roof
and its *maçaranduba* frame.

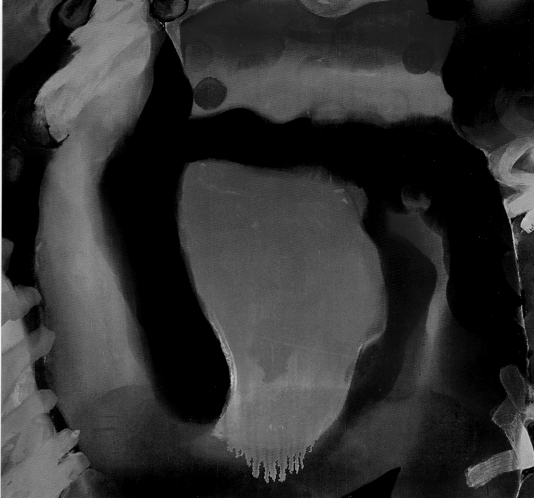

ABOVE, LEFT Made of an authentic timber from Amazonia—the *maçaranduba*—,
the frame is entirely clad in bamboo. Though familiar with the material,
this tour de force constituted a challenge to the local craftsmen.
ABOVE, RIGHT, AND FACING PAGE The works of art displayed in the rooms are
for the most part by artist friends of the owner, such as Vik Muniz,
Charles Watson, Amalia Giacomini, and Nelson Felix.
FOLLOWING DOUBLE PAGE Sculpture by Brazilian artist Ricardo Ventura.

The style and placement of the furniture are relatively informal, with the accent placed on family pastimes and entertaining, in true Carioca fashion.

PRECEDING DOUBLE PAGE The plan of the house could hardly be simpler. The double-pitch roof rests on wooden pillars. Sculpture by Artur Lescher.

FACING PAGE The large rooms boast bay windows that seem to bring the forest and its fauna inside. Cushions by Italian designer Lisa Corti.

ABOVE The couple who owns the house adores entertaining. The cheeses are handmade by the hostess.

Ricardo Nauenberg's Tropical Retreat

"Rio de Janeiro is the only conurbation I know that has not succeeded in halting nature at its gates. Here we live among the sea, the mountains, the rainforest that from all sides tumbles its mangos and palms into the bottom of our gardens, into our very houses." **Paul Claudel**, *L'Œil écoute*, 1946.

City and nature are almost synonymous in Rio de Janeiro. The landmarks used by Cariocas are all natural, the districts being located with reference to Corcovado, the Pedra de Gávea, or the forest of Tijuca. For architects who work there, the chief issue is precisely to how integrate their constructions into such a flourishing environment.

Climbing up to Viola da Boa Vista, one comes upon a house standing amid the greenery, an unfinished project by the late Cláudio Bernardes. An adept of vertical lines and with a marked preference for wood, iron, stone, and concrete, the architect declared that the simpler the plan, the better the result. The terrain proved to be a springboard for a construction whose sole limits are its unpredictable and organic contours.

All the rooms of this house communicate with the world outside. Daylight pours into the interior space through a central glass ceiling. The whole edifice can only be appreciated by taking into account the all-important interaction between light, wind, and sun. From the inside, all the spaces turn toward the exterior that enters in through generous windows and great glass doors. All the forms seem to spring from the materials from which they were made and unfold naturally, and harmoniously.

The plan is simple. The ground floor includes a living room, dining room, and kitchen, and is flanked by the swimming pool and the gardens. Out on the terrace, wooden seats and deckchairs invite one to gaze out over a spectacular view of the mountain and the trees. The iron staircase in the center with wooden steps and a discreet steel-wire and wood rail leads to the floor above where the bedrooms and the office are located. In the middle of the house stands the trunk of a tall tree that rises up to the glazed canopy with all four sides of the exposed roof stretching out like great branches that shelter the rooms below. The walls on the ground floor are composed of large glass panels held in place by green-painted iron columns, all but eliminating any boundary with the forest and opening the space up to infinity. The armature of the roof barely brushes the columns, seeming instead to float in the light filtering down through the tops of the surrounding trees.

The feeling of relaxation and freedom is total and, so far from the hustle and bustle, one forgets one is in a city. That is Rio: in osmosis with nature, its most glorious asset. ≋

FACING PAGE This residence is in fact an unfinished project by Cláudio Bernardes, an architect particularly committed to making dwellings that fit in with their surroundings. The chief aim of his initial plan was to integrate nature into the future construction.

In the middle of the house stands the trunk of
a tall tree that rises up to the glazed canopy,
with all four sides of the exposed roof stretching out
like great branches sheltering the rooms below.

PRECEDING DOUBLE PAGE, AND FACING PAGE The great tree trunk standing
in the middle of the house supports all four sides of a roof dressed
in bamboo braided with a geometrical pattern. The glass canopy
at the center of the space lets the sunlight flood into the interior.
ABOVE Photographs by Ricardo Nauenberg.
FOLLOWING DOUBLE PAGE The ground floor is lined entirely with glass
panels to benefit from the daylight.
PAGES 232-33 AND 234-35 The chairs and wooden deckchairs out on
the terrace are the ideal spot for gazing out over the glorious vista.

Between the Mountains and the Sea: a Villa in São Conrado

Rio de Janeiro has grown up between mountain and ocean. With one's back to the sea, the eye can follow the line of hills enclosing the city. São Conrado is the district where forest, mountain, and ocean converge. Its two summits, Pedra Bonita and Pedra de Gávea, are landmarks for Cariocas and meccas for adepts of hang-gliding and rock climbing. It was in this part of town, that, in 1990, architects Cláudio Bernardes and Paulo Jacobsen designed a truly spectacular house.

They envisaged a house with as few solid walls as possible so as to remain open to the magnificent scenery beyond. Enhanced by a ground plan based on parallel lines, an illusion of infinite space transpires in each and every detail. It is as though the architects' only instruments in realizing their idea that the inner space should shoot off to infinity are the straight edge and the set square. All sense of distance dissolves into the blue of the sky, the sea, and the refreshing pool behind the house.

As if by magic, when the door opens, the entrance to the house—nestled in a tropical garden planted with bromeliads, mangos, and a vast panoply of local plants—is bathed in natural light. The eye is torn between the vast living room and the wooden staircase leading down to the lower floor, the saw-like pattern formed by the steps being interrupted only by the flood of daylight reflected up from the bottom of the swimming pool. The living area and swimming pool stretch out as if to the horizon. The former is adorned with Brazilian and international contemporary artworks whose colors offer a joyous counterpoint to the natural world beyond, while the chairs are painted in a range of blues which, when the retractable roof opens above the dining table, echo the sky above.

The rest of the house radiates from the large sitting room through the space of the swimming pool. Sea and vegetation are an integral part of the decor; the green marble chosen for the bathroom seems organic and it is hard to identify where the cladding stops and the forest begins. The seemingly endless wooden staircase leads to a corridor that serves the bedrooms and the family room. To temper the rectilinear layout, warmth is provided by sizable wooden panels covering the walls.

The feeling of freedom and spaciousness filling the house is in perfect accord with the hang-gliders and paragliders seen taking off from Pedra Bonita or landing on the beach of São Conrado opposite. ≋

FACING PAGE Cláudio Bernardes and Paulo Jacobsen's plan is a remarkable illustration of the quest for a perfect balance between nature and modern architecture.
FOLLOWING DOUBLE PAGE The vast living room is separated from the swimming pool by two large glazed doors; the metal-frame roof canopy allows the light to flood into the entire room, though it is also fitted with bands of plaited fiber for a more subdued effect.

ABOVE, RIGHT, AND FACING PAGE Such luminosity allows palm trees and other tropical species to grow even inside the house. Works by international artists are to be found beneath the double-height ceilings, but the contemporary spirit makes itself felt in every object and every piece of furniture.
FOLLOWING DOUBLE PAGE The master bathroom benefits from an outdoor Italian-style shower and a marble-dressed bathtub.

240

The pattern formed by the steps is interrupted only by the flood of daylight reflected down through the bottom of the swimming pool overhead.

ABOVE AND FACING PAGE On the terrace, the infinity pool forms a watery link between ocean and sky. The glass bottom allows the light to penetrate down to the large wooden staircase leading to the living areas.

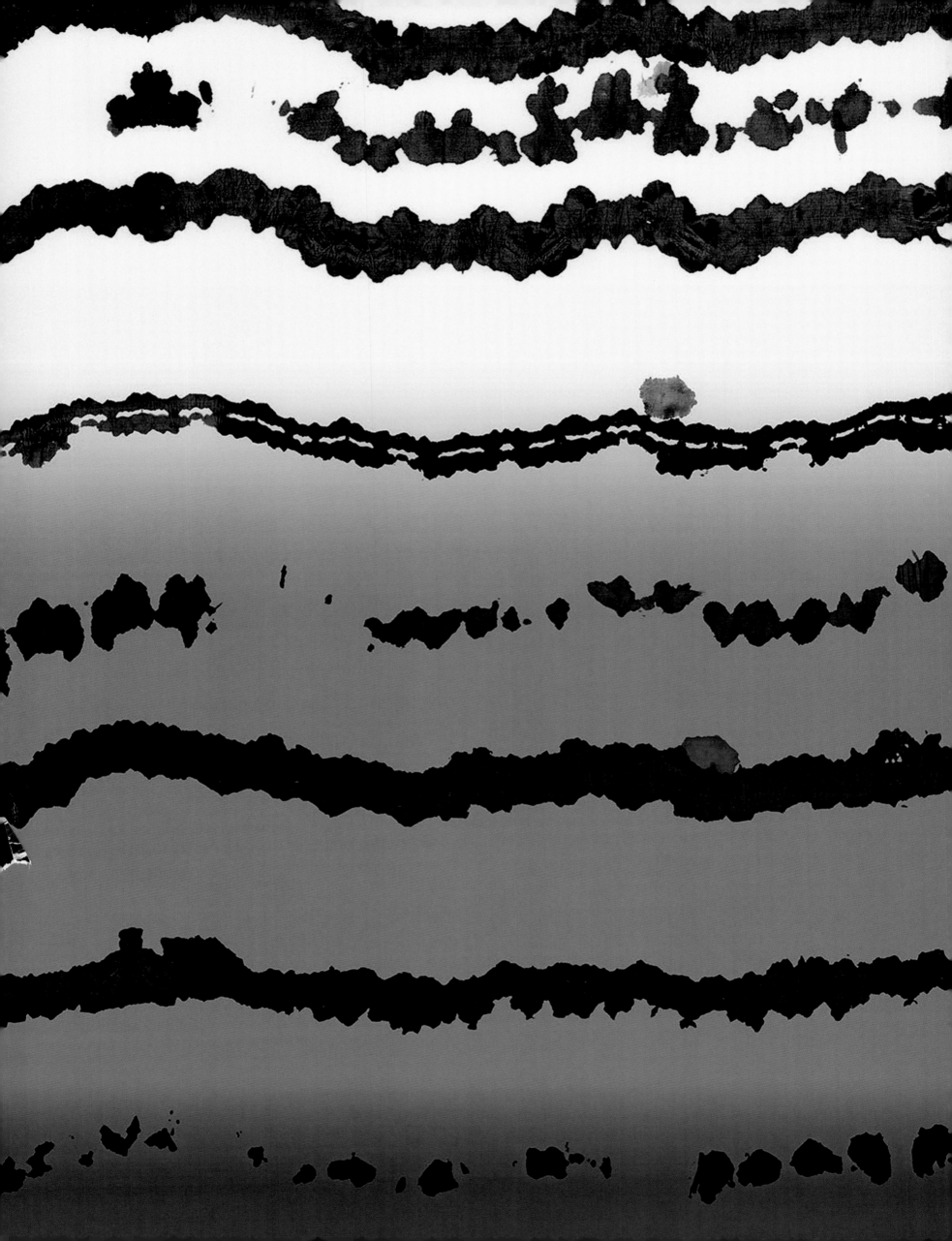

MODERNIST HOUSES

Classic Modernity
at Mount Corcovado

"When I designed the residence some forty years ago in 1970,
I took care to make it a structure that could survive time and remain timeless.
It is a joy to see that after so many years the house is still up to date."
Luiz Eduardo Índio da Costa, 2012.

Rio de Janeiro sits at the crossroads between mountain, forest, and the Atlantic, and one of its most traditional quarters has grown up around the Botanical Gardens. It was in 1808, following a journey to Brazil by the Portuguese imperial family, that the prince regent, João VI, dazzled by the tropical flora, decided to dedicate a garden to its treasures. The house by architect Luis Eduardo Índio da Costa standing at the foot of Mount Corcovado—the pedestal of one of the seven modern wonders of the world, the statue of Christ the Redeemer—is the quintessence of Rio, with its proximity to the ocean, mountains, and nature.

The harmony between architecture and scenery here is exemplary; concrete columns stand next to palm trees, the tropical garden slopes in from the forest of Tijuca to blend calmly and subtly with the building, while the great picture windows ensure that the superb natural scenery enhances the artworks the owners have collected inside. The interior—a comfortable paragon of contemporary style—presents a contrasting, yet harmonious blend of classical and modern. The white façade surges up from the entryway, framed by straight lines in exposed concrete, but tempered by the innumerable tones of green in the garden and splashes of color from the flowers. Windows and generously glazed doors open all over the structure, imparting a bold sense of rhythm with their broad wooden bars.

Harmony is the keynote within the residence too: the rooms are embellished with works by Brazilian artists such as Candido Portinari, Emiliano Di Cavalcanti, Amílcar de Castro, Bruno Giorgi, Sérgio de Camargo, Tunga, and Beatriz Milhazes, all of which rub shoulders with eighteenth-century furniture, European, Chinese or modern porcelain, and altar hangings, all ravishingly displayed.

The Bordeaux-red painted walls in the dining room match the trimming on the Dom José-style chairs in jacaranda wood; a silver candelabrum and twisted columns impart a note of simplicity. The colors of the crystal and the crockery, and the delicate motifs of the European porcelain contribute to the atmosphere, reflecting the splashes of daylight flooding in from the garden.

In the garden, the blue shimmer of the swimming pool reflects that of the sky, reaching out to the Rodrigo de Freitas Lagoon and, beyond, to the beach of Ipanema. Among this daze of blues and greens, the shady trees cast long shadows on a lawn dedicated to fun and relaxation.

Rio de Janeiro is like that: art and architecture blend and merge, and nature is the center. ≈≈

FACING PAGE Mount Corcovado and Christ the Redeemer form the background to this splendid villa built up on the heights of the city near the Botanical Gardens.

ABOVE Surrounded on all sides by the richly verdant garden, the side wall disappears beneath a coat of dense, climbing plants through which peep various species of orchids.
FACING PAGE Nestling in a gorgeous natural setting, this villa designed by architect Luis Eduardo Índio da Costa seems timeless—at once modern and classic.

Among this daze of blues and greens,
the shady trees cast long shadows on a manicured
lawn dedicated to fun and relaxation.

FACING PAGE Windows and generously glazed doors open all over
the structure, imparting a sense of rhythm with their broad wooden
bars and providing the construction with its distinct architectonic style.
ABOVE Perfect harmony reigns between art and nature,
which here seem to be as one.
FOLLOWING DOUBLE PAGE From the garden and the swimming pool one
can admire pieces from the contemporary sculpture collection and
delight in the panoramic view.

ABOVE The interior of the house features a fine collection of Brazilian art; modern works, such as this painting by Amilcar de Castro, are joined by furniture from the eighteenth and nineteenth centuries.

FACING PAGE, BOTTOM The jacaranda wood chairs in the dining room are eighteenth century. On the table, the light from the silver chandelier and candelabra shimmers over Baccarat-crystal glasses in various colors. Typical Brazilian silver amulets accompany the European porcelain and china from the East India Company. Sunlight comes in through a French window flanked by two Solomonic column stands.

FOLLOWING DOUBLE PAGE The tall palms form the plant equivalents of concrete columns.

In the Japanese Style: a Seaside Villa in Joatinga

José Zanine Caldas was born on the southern coast of Bahia. At age twenty, he moved to Rio to start an architectural scale model workshop. In this context, he met Oscar Niemeyer and Lucio Costa, who invited him to work on the construction of Brazil's capital Brasília. He began to explore his own reinterpretation of architecture in the 1960s. Forsaking reinforced concrete and steel, he began to create dwellings made of wood and stone that took their cue entirely from nature. He was a pioneer, recycling wooden doors and windows in his constructions, and paving the way to neo-rustic and ecological architecture. Showing special respect for the environment, each volume in this house in Joatinga has literally been sculpted out of the surrounding rock.

Built in 1966 on a cliff above the city, it seems to perch on the stone. From the street outside one can even glimpse a patch of sky between house and rock. Nothing obstructs the view of the house over the sea and the horizon. The house displays an uncompromising horizontality despite the steep terrain on which it sits, and blends influences from Brazilian colonial style, with its high ceilings and exposed tiles, with the kind of interlocking planes typical of the architecture of Japan, whence Zanine Caldas had returned shortly prior to designing the house.

Conceived for a tropical climate, the plan of the building allows air to circulate through all the rooms, while the swimming pool placed on the stone that encroaches into the central living room cools the entire dwelling. Beyond the living room that gives onto the street and the sea, the colorful transition of an immaculate lawn leads the eye unimpeded to the horizon, while the great beams crisscrossing the roof add further to the feeling of spaciousness.

All the furniture in the living area was also designed by the architect and forms an integral part of the dwelling; it seems almost as though the massive blocks of wood have been hewn with a single blow into settees, tables, and benches. The dining room on the level above the main room offers an unimpeded vista over the ocean. The table was also designed by the architect, who decorated the top with eighteenth-century *azulejos*. To the sides of the property, the bedrooms are carved out of the rock and glazed with vast panes that open onto the sea. The doors, windows, and balusters were rescued from the Rio portside when the Lloyd Brasileiro warehouses were demolished in the 1960s.

Color plays a significant role in providing the house with its unity. The prevailing note is inevitably given by blue since the sea and sky fill each of the house's strategically placed openings, forming an integral part of the color scheme. The tropical greenery surrounding and sheltering the house contrasts with the wood brackets of its heavy frame. Painted yellow, the recycled doors and the cement patio facing the swimming pool reflect and draw in the sunlight.

Zanine Caldas sold the house in 1971 to the economist and art dealer Mauricio Leite Barbosa who has respectfully preserved the house and its original furniture.

A tribute to the beauty of Rio de Janeiro, this sparsely decorated house bears witness to the owners' respect for the surrounding landscape. ≋

FACING PAGE Created by José Zanine Caldas, the gossamer timber frame of the Joatinga house transforms the structure into a work of art. The construction seems to be suspended above the rock, leaving the air and light free to circulate all around.
FOLLOWING DOUBLE PAGE AND PAGES 264-65 The residence offers a perfect illustration of a blend of the Brazilian colonial style and the architecture of Japan, from where Zanine Caldas had recently returned when he began sketching the house's plans.

PRECEDING DOUBLE PAGE, ABOVE, AND FACING PAGE The furniture was
designed by the architect. Positioned to keep the space free
and open, the wooden and leather couches are fixed to the
floor. The room extends out to the horizon: nothing is allowed
to obstruct the view over the vast ocean. The dining room is
on a different level from the lounge, standing on a rock that
gives the swimming pool encroaching into the lounge
its characteristic shape.

268

A Modernist Masterpiece

"It is not the right angle that attracts me. Nor the straight line, tough, inflexible, created by man. What attracts me is the free, sensual curve. The curve I find in the mountains of my country, in the sinuous course of its rivers, in the waves of the sea, in the clouds of the sky, in the body of the favorite woman. Of curves is made all the universe, the curved universe of Einstein." **Oscar Niemeyer**

Rua Canoas offers one of the most attractive walks in all Rio de Janeiro. Leaving São Conrado, one enters the forest of Tijuca, coming out at Alto da Boa Vista. It is here, in the midst of the most luxuriant scenery, that Oscar Niemeyer built his home.

His primary concern was to leave the environment intact: rocks protrude into the living room, and sweeping curves and organic forms run through the house over the uneven terrain. Luxuriant vegetation too, with an exuberance no straight line can curtail, claims pride of place. Designed in 1951 and completed in 1953, the Canoas House pays homage to Brazilian culture and traditions, while leaving the architect totally free to organize the space as he wished and make the most of the existing natural elements.

The hand of the master is evident throughout the building: reinforced concrete, flagstones borne on slender columns, extensive glass panels, and sinuous overlapping lines, as in the swimming pool that extends over the roof. This continuity of line is so marked that one cannot always tell whether one is inside the house or out. Such architectural flair has no need of decoration: it is a work of art by itself. Oscar Niemeyer's home is a synthesis of all modern architecture, whose overriding characteristic is freedom of expression. The house's garden is simply the forest surrounding it: it emerges from nature, sheltered by age-old trees.

In 2007, in time for the architect's hundredth birthday, the house was placed on the National Historical and Cultural Heritage list and today forms part of the Niemeyer Foundation. Prolific in Brazil—the most striking example being of course Brasília—and all over the globe, Niemeyer forged the architectural identity of his homeland. Moreover, this man, as unique as his art, has left his house open to the public, so that both Brazilians and visitors from faraway can here meditate on his conception of life. ≈

FACING PAGE Built in the 1950s by Oscar Niemeyer on the Estrada das Canoas, this house was originally the architect's home. In 2007, in honor of the hundredth anniversary of his birth, it was listed as part of the national historic and artistic heritage; it today houses the Oscar Niemeyer Foundation and can be visited by appointment.

"My work doesn't matter; for me, architecture doesn't matter. What does is life, the fact that people meet, embrace, show solidarity, dream up a better world. The rest is just words." **Oscar Niemeyer**

Rocks protrude into the living room, and sweeping
curves and organic forms run through the house
over the uneven terrain.

PRECEDING DOUBLE PAGE AND ABOVE The architect's overriding concern
was to fully integrate the house into its environment; a large
rock emerges inside the building on the swimming pool's edge.
The walls are transparent, the residence being surrounded
by vast panels of glass. The interior opens out onto the
swimming pool, thereby blurring the limit between outside and
in. Sculptures by Alfredo Ceschiatti stand about the garden.

FACING PAGE The paving inside continues to the edge
of the swimming pool, extending the space and
erasing all sense of division among the architectural
features of the site.

FACING PAGE AND ABOVE Oscar Niemeyer designed most of the house's furniture himself, except the chairs in the dining room, where he opted for the curved forms of the classic Thonet favored by many architects of the period.

A Rustic Elegance

High above Joatinga beach, this superb residence was born from the meeting between Zanine Caldas and Hélio Pellegrino. José Zanine Caldas, landscape designer, sculptor, furniture designer, and self-taught architect, worked both in Brazil and abroad. His talent, combined with a profound knowledge of the natural world, earned him international recognition and even a nickname: the "Master of Wood."

At the end of the 1960s, Zanine Caldas settled in Rio de Janeiro, where he built dozens of houses in the district of Joatinga, a district situated between São Conrado and the Barra da Tijuca. He left his mark there with architecture centered on the concept of self-construction, at once colonial and modern and built out of environmentally friendly materials. Standing in a Joatinga condominium this house is a prime example of the architectural vision of Zanine Caldas. Simplicity in conception allied to an unwavering concern for nature results in a rustic type of dwelling, a veritable architectonic sculpture where no wall obstructs the view of the surrounding landscape, the space being divided instead by large glass panels or arrangements of wooden spheres. The architect's overriding intention was to make as little impact as possible on the site. Operating like a builder of yesteryear, he traced a life-size plan on the plot into which the foundation piles were set and the floors laid over a terrain left unleveled.

In the 1990s, alterations were made by a new owner, who turned to architect Hélio Pellegrino, another specialist in environmental protection and in the reuse of wood and demolition materials. Also a visual artist and decorator, Hélio Pellegrino marshalled all his diverse talents to transform the walls, floors, and ceilings into works of art combining bottles, pot shards, hydraulic tiles, terra-cotta, stone, and cement. For Hélio Pellegrino, a home must reflect the lifestyle of its occupant. Into Zanine Caldas's original concept he thus incorporated a gym and a brick corridor that borders the tennis court and swimming pool of the earlier design. The latter extends into a garden arranged over two levels, creating the illusion of a waterfall that echoes the spectacle of the sea off the Barra da Tijuca. To the side of the exercise room, a second swimming pool nestles in a Japanese-style landscape contrasting with the palm trees and the giant bromeliads in the garden.

In this way, the house manages to integrate the talents of two masters of architecture, two precursors of green concerns and of the recycling of quality materials. But neither was satisfied with just creating the volumes; they also designed the furniture and many other elements in the house, so that the whole appears to have emerged from one and the same burst of creative energy. ≈

FACING PAGE The wooden door with its casing and steps in dressed stone produces a monumental effect to the entrance.
FOLLOWING DOUBLE PAGE When the house was sold, Zanine Caldas' original plans were reworked and completed by Hélio Pellegrino. Both architects shared the same love of nature and used recycled building materials.

ABOVE, RIGHT, AND FACING PAGE The glass panels across the back
facade allow daylight to flood the interior. *Opus incertum*
paves both the courtyard and the living room floor.
The main entrance is planted with giant bromeliads
and other tropical plants.

ARTISTS' STUDIOS

Antonio Mello Mourão's Studio in an Urban Forest

Just coincidence? The studio of Antonio Mello Mourão, known as Tunga, one of the most important contemporary Brazilian artists, was designed by the "Master of Wood," Marta Alencar, who collaborated with José Zanine Caldas. Tunga and Zanine Caldas enjoy an international reputation. The architect had works exhibited in the Louvre at the end of the 1980s and in 2004–05 the same museum showed Tunga's installation *By the Light of Two Worlds*.

Enveloped by the forest in the Barra Tijuca quarter, the studio is conceived as a sculpture. First and foremost, it respects the environment—the rocks and the rugged terrain in which stand pieces of understated sculpturality. Its vast volumes are traversed by rustic wooden beams, creating a sequence of overlapping planes; panels of glass do away with all sense of visual divide.

Presented out in the garden as well as inside the studio, Tunga's works seem to be an emanation of nature: metal braids and magnets recall creepers twisting round trees; the spheres of *Tesouro Besouro* ("treasure of the dung-beetle") are inspired by the balls of organic material rolled before them by certain coleopterans in the north of Brazil.

The vast, transformable interior spaces are interconnected by staircases. A glass ceiling in the center of the roof floods them with light, giving an open-air feel. The subtle colors of the decor and the materials in which the sculptures are made offer a delicate foil to what is an artistic, but working environment.

Tunga produced his first works in the 1970s. His drawings and sculptures refer abundantly to literature, art, philosophy, and science—archaeology, paleontology, zoology, and medicine—and testify to his ceaseless capacity for research and the complexity of his creative world. As an artist, he was strongly influenced by Hélio Oiticica and Lygia Clark, initiators in the 1960s of Brazilian neo-concretism.

All Marta Alencar's realizations correspond to the Zanine Caldas' fundamental tenet: *it is the landscape that counts. The house should enter into an interrelationship with everything that surrounds it, not to distort it, not to force it; it should give the impression of always having been there.* For Tunga, sculpture embodies enigmatic forms and figures whose strangeness and fabulous proportions perplex, and upset our everyday perceptions of near and far, of inside and out, of full and void. The importance he accords the unconscious and the associations of the dream lead him to create multifaceted, highly complex works.

The two artists seem to intersect at this very spot: Marta Alencar planning, dimensioning, harmonizing; Tunga transforming, distorting, completing, and together recreating their single object of study: nature. ≈≈

FACING PAGE The place that Antonio Mello Mourão, known as Tunga, chose for his studio testifies to his great respect for nature. It is in this house designed by another artist, Marta Alencar, that he creates the majority of his works.

TOP, FACING PAGE, AND FOLLOWING DOUBLE PAGE The different open spaces are linked by stairways, while the glass canopy in the center of the roof bathes everything in natural light. **BOTTOM** The artist's sculptures are displayed in the garden. Metal braiding and spheres from the series *Tesouros Besouro*, realized in the 1990s, create an exotic landscape in the surrounding luxuriant vegetation.

Brazilian Exuberance:
Beatriz Milhazes' Studio

Standing on the fringes of the lagoon of Rodrigo de Freitas, the park of the Botanical Gardens is one of the most splendid survivors from the regency of João VI. Created as a staging post to acclimatize spice trees from the Indies and today housing rare specimens of tropical flora, it was inaugurated in June 1808, receiving the royal title of the "Real Horto Botânico" in October of the same year. Developing in the nineteenth and early twentieth centuries, the surrounding area evolved into one of the most delightful quarters in all Rio de Janeiro; it is extremely well preserved, and one can still find whole streets of historic semi-detached houses.

It is in one of these streets that Beatriz Milhazes has set up her studio. Passers-by might never suspect that this house contains the work of an artist famous not just in Brazil but all over the world. With its generous windows and warm wooden floorboards, the first floor is peaceful and welcoming. Nature has her place in the courtyard garden, while brightly colored works by the artist are arranged on the walls as the fancy takes her. Above the desk, a panel serves as an autobiographical album covered with the artist's pictures and souvenirs.

Beatriz Milhazes entered the Parque Lage School of the Visual Arts in 1980, later teaching and coordinating its Painting Department. In 1984, she took part in the exhibition: "How are you, Generation '80?" her name becoming synonymous with a group of artists then revitalizing the Brazilian art scene.

Beatriz Milhazes' work expresses a number of formal concerns inherent in the history of abstract painting, from Henri Matisse's vibrant colors to the rigorous structural compositions of Piet Mondrian. Color is incidentally the structural element of her work. Rosettes, pearls, flowers, arabesques, and lacework teem over the paintings, which, over the course of time and with maturity, testify to her enduring talent as a colorist. She has developed a technique relying on the principle of collage. She begins her works by painting the motifs on a plastic sheet and which is then glued on the canvas and removes the plastic sheet like a decal. Her paintings are made of these small pieces painted separately and placed together, creating a multitude of layers. The sheets are stamped with a memory, and their use may lead to irregularities. Beatriz Milhazes works paint into an infinite range of shades, with no fear of contrast. Yet, magically, on the canvas, all these tones complement one another.

There is an amazing amount of creativity, exuberance of form and hue in this unassuming early twentieth-century attic room. Blotches of color, static forms, and virgin canvases can spark movement or define a composition. All that it awaits is a stroke from the artist's brush to come alive. ≈

FACING PAGE The simplicity and sparseness of Beatriz Milhazes's studio in the vicinity of the Botanical Gardens makes it the ideal place for her painting centered on color. Large ongoing canvases hang on every white wall in the serene house.

Nature has its place in the courtyard garden,
while brightly colored works by the artist
are arranged on the walls as the fancy takes her.

ABOVE AND FACING PAGE With its metal structure and wooden
steps, the staircase on the broad stone wall at the
back could itself be a sculpture. The dazzlingly colorful
paintings echo the shades of green in the interior garden.

FACING PAGE AND ABOVE Flowers and arabesques, circles, targets, and squares take form as the artist builds up paint on the canvas. Beatriz Milhazes also makes collages out of material from daily life and clippings, recreated using her artist's eye.

Design and Modernity at Ricardo Fasanello's Studio

Santa Teresa is one of the most traditional districts in Rio. Its superb situation on the heights of the "Serra Carioca" gives it a commanding view of almost the entire city. Its irregularly paved streets are a throwback to the eighteenth century. Through it runs the famous electric tram, the *bondo*, a popular means of transport and the district's most characteristic hallmark. The quarter also plays host to some of the most venerable churches in the city. It is in this *bairro*, in front of the church of Nossa Senhora das Neves ("Our Lady of the Snows") that designer Ricardo Fasanello chose to set up his workshop.

Born in São Paulo, Ricardo was something of a child prodigy: when just fourteen, he had already designed and built a boat. Settling in Rio at age eighteen, he started working with new materials, such as resin, leather, wood, steel, and fiberglass. Exploiting the plasticity of these substances in the raw, he created a multitude of daring, avant-garde forms.

His studio was a research laboratory, where the ergonomics of curves, spheres, circles, and cylinders were mathematically explored and applied to improve the comfort of the user, the aesthetic constant being a reference to speed and to the car engine—the artist's great passion.

The "Fardos" easy-chair, comprised of three large leather cylinders sat one on top of the other, was his first international hit, being exhibited in Paris in 1971 and then in Berlin.

Although a child of the 1960s and '70s, the artist's Santa Teresa workshop remains a temple of modernity. Located on a slope amid the trees, it has the feeling of being both a haven of relaxation and a busy place of work. While the great picture window giving on to the old city extends the space, the arched ceiling dressed with wooden slats is more reminiscent of a tent. Everything here bears the stamp of the lifestyle chosen by the artist. The workshop is as relevant today as when it was built more than fifty years ago, thanks to Ricardo Fasanello's conception of comfort. The workshop where the artist's plans were turned into resin and steel molds is located a matter of yards from the studio, while the leather elements are still handcrafted on the spot.

Although Ricardo Fasanello died prematurely in 1993, his studio remains active, being devoted primarily to restoring and repairing his pieces. Everywhere are set squares, drawing boards, tools, and personal articles—all conceived and made by Ricardo. As evening draws in and the sun starts to descend, its fading light dappling through the tree tops, it is easy to see why the artist chose this place. Surrounded by the organic forms of his art, one positively breathes wellbeing and ease. The two keynotes of Ricardo Fasanello's inspiration are style and quality of life. These he made eternal, and they still afford delight to the astonished visitor in every room of his workshop. ≈

FACING PAGE AND FOLLOWING DOUBLE PAGE The place where Ricardo Fasanello designed and built his furniture originally served as a veritable research laboratory. It was here that the artist drew, constructed, and tested his creations. He was especially interested in novel materials, with which he created the curved lines, lightness, and comfort associated with his name.

ABOVE AND FACING PAGE Pieces exhibited in the workshop include leather-clad fiberglass *Esfera* ("sphere") armchairs, steel *Anel* ("ring") chair and armchair with leather seats and backs, the *Gaivota* ("gull") chair, and the *Fardos* ("balls") fireside armchair.

304   INSIDE RIO

PALACES AND VILLAS

A Legendary Hotel:
The Copacabana Palace

"Finally the arc of the beach appears, an enchanting vision: on the broadwalk
ceaselessly whipped by seething waves, with its houses, villas, and gardens
one can already clearly make out the grand hotel and, on the hillside, houses
surrounded by the forest. But no! For this was just the beach at Copacabana,
one of most beautiful in the world, simply a new suburb, and not the city itself."
Stefan Zweig, "A Short Trip through Brazil", 1936.

With its face turned resolutely to the Atlantic Ocean, Copacabana is one of the most beautiful and best-known beaches in all Rio de Janeiro. Featured in many a *bossa nova* as the "princess of the sea," for Cariocas it remains a place teeming with possibilities. As the first district in the bay of Guanabara to undergo serious development, the earliest buildings date from the end of the nineteenth century.

By the 1920s, Rio was already the federal district capital, yet it was still essentially a seaside resort. In 1923 the local elite turned its proximity to the sea to good account by building this eminently grand "Grand Hotel." The owners, the Guinles awarded the contract for its construction to Joseph Gire, a French architect who had already worked for the family. Guests from the world over promptly flocked to an establishment that provided the perfect springboard for discovering the natural beauties of the city. Period photographs show the beach with a handful of houses on the broadwalk and a majestic building in the style of a French resort towering over them. Gire took his inspiration from the Carlton Hotel in Cannes and Nice's Negresco, and the Copacabana Palace soon imposed its status as Rio de Janeiro's traditional deluxe hotel *par excellence*.

In 1940s and '50s, Rio high society congregated in the "Copa," as it was familiarly called, and ever since, members of royal houses, stars of screen, theater, music, and sport, as well as politicians and business people, have continued to arrive in droves to delight in its refinement, impeccable service, and unique location on the world-famous beach front. The Copacabana Palace acquired international fame after Fred Astaire and Ginger Rogers danced there in the film *Flying Down to Rio*. Its glamourous reception halls, its delectable Golden Room, and its auditorium have played host many memorable shows and functions.

But the Copacabana Palace also plays a part in the life of every Carioca, whether it was the venue for their wedding reception or because they spent an hour or two there waiting for the autograph of their favorite star.

In 1989, the Guinles sold the hotel, but fortunately the renovation undertaken by Orient-Express Hotels Ltd. has left its timeless style and welcoming ambiance intact. Standing proudly at the center of the great sweep of the beach, the Copa continues to extend its invitation to passers-by on the Avenida Atlântica, forming the ideal venue to relax for a moment and savor one of the prettiest views of Rio de Janeiro or look out over the ultramarine vastness of the sea. ≈

FACING PAGE AND FOLLOWING DOUBLE PAGE Opened in 1923, the Copacabana was designed by the French architect Joseph Gire. Inspired by the architecture of the French Riviera, it is reminiscent of the Negresco in Nice and the Carlton in Cannes. Now an integral part of Carioca life, it was in its time the first grand hotel on the seafront.

ABOVE, FACING PAGE, AND FOLLOWING DOUBLE PAGE The swimming pool to the side of the hotel is one of the most delightful places to spend time here. The pergola and the passageway lead through to the Cipriani Restaurant, where classic Italian cuisine goes hand in hand with Murano glass lamps and Venetian mirrors.

312   INSIDE RIO

FACING PAGE AND ABOVE The sweep and boardwalk of Copacabana beach can be seen from the balconies of the rooms over the Avenida Atlântica. The Copacabana is surely the most typically deluxe hotel in Rio and it holds a special place in the hearts of all Cariocas.

Deco Deluxe: an Art Deco Treasure in Santa Teresa

Rising imperial palms inexorably draw the eye to a splendid residence standing to the rear of a large garden. It was designed by the Austrian architect Josej Pitilk and commissioned by another European, Arnst Thun, a botanist and coffee wholesaler, who in 1920 purchased a plot with a modest house that he busied himself upscaling into a veritable little palace. In the 1930s, the family of Monteiro de Carvalho bought the property and, after a number of alterations, started building what is today considered an art deco gem.

The patriarch, Alberto Monteiro de Carvalho, was an engineer and architect who trained at prestigious and innovative Polytechnic School of the University of São Paulo. In 1906, he became deeply intrigued by the work of Otto Wagner and the Vienna School, in new techniques and materials, and in contemporary taste more generally. Soon he established links with many of the Europeans and Americans who imposed pure lines and advanced technological solutions on the architecture of the twentieth century.

In the 1920s he discovered the art of René Lalique, whom he met at the Paris Exhibition of 1925. Dazzled by the designer's stylized, geometrical lines, he began to imagine a house of his own in the same manner. Ten years later, for the dining room, he placed an order with the Maison Lalique for the "Dahlia" chandelier, and for ceiling lights and sconces that had decorated the pavilion at the Exhibition. They are all described in the voluminous series of letters exchanged at that time. In fact Lalique was to furnish not only the light fittings, but also ornamental objects and the great satin-finish frosted glass table placed in the center of the hall that separates the reception room from the library and office.

Other, mainly French designers also lent a hand: Jean Perzel, Mario Sabino, Degues, and the firm of Baguès, with whom a similarly extensive correspondence was struck up concerning orders that were each to be an exclusive work of art. Similar care was lavished on the selection of the furniture. At the wrought-iron workshop of Borderel and Robert, and Alberto struck up an acquaintance with their creative director Raymond Subes. It was he who designed the chairs in the wintergarden, as well as other pieces of furniture like the metal consoles and dressers. Subes also received a commission for the large door separating the dining room and the wintergarden which was finally designed by Alberto himself. The cabinetmakers Leleu and Dominique also figure among the many designers who turned this residence into a veritable museum of the French art deco style, whose elegance and sophistication it embodies so wonderfully. Alberto Monteiro de Carvalho's genius lies in having foreseen that what was contemporary in his day would over time become a classic. And indeed it is this style that to this day is synonymous with modernity.

This opulent abode could be in any metropolis and have been designed for anyone of taste. As the Monteiro de Carvalho family had it built in Rio, it houses all their objects and art works, as well as an abundant collection of archives that brings back to life a long-lost era and also reminds one of the skill of the craftsmen who contributed to making Casa Monteiro de Carvalho what it is today.

Fly down to Rio, then, if you have a love of art deco! ≋

FACING PAGE The superb semi-circular porch to the side of the edifice, with its checkerboard marble flooring, marble stairs, and a pair of bronze Great Danes—reproductions of the ones in the château at Chantilly by the great French *animalier* sculptor Gardet.

Alberto Monteiro de Carvalho became one of
the major patrons of the French luxury industries
during the 1920s and 1930s.

FACING PAGE, ABOVE, AND FOLLOWING DOUBLE PAGE The walls of the vestibule connecting
the library to the drawingroom are lined with wood paneling. The painting is
by Vicente do Rego Monteiro. Lalique's frosted-crystal cat is just one beast
from the residence's abundant glass menagerie.

PRECEDING DOUBLE PAGE Every room in the residence offers a trip back in time; all the furniture, every single object tells a story.
ABOVE AND FACING PAGE The dining room boasts Lalique "Dahlia" lighting; the central chandelier was made-to-measure. The superb reception hall presents an exceptional series of vases by Gallé; a collection of porcelain soup tureens by the Companhia das Índias being the other high point. The console tables are exclusive creations by Raymond Subes. Other extraordinary examples of art deco furniture include pieces signed by cabinetmakers Leleu and Dominique.

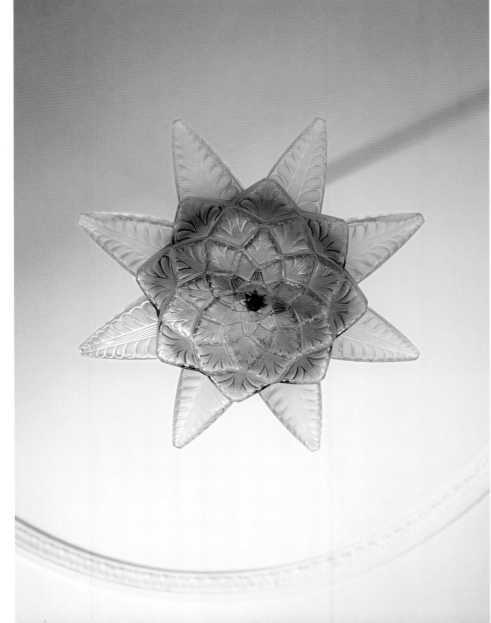

The owner's genius lies in having foreseen that what was contemporary in his day would over time become a classic. And indeed it is this style that to this day is synonymous with modernity.

ABOVE AND FACING PAGE The furniture in the wintergarden adjacent to the dining room was made entirely to designs by Raymond Subes. The sconces are by Jean Perzel, who created them in 1935 for the Palace of the League of Nations in Geneva.

FOLLOWING DOUBLE PAGE Towering imperial palms look down on visitors as they make their way to the splendid residence at the back of the garden.

A Residence in the Art Nouveau Style: the Laranjeiras Palace

"Surrounding one overwhelmingly on all sides is not the inexhaustible diversity of beings and things, but a single awe-inspiring presence: The New World."
Claude Lévi-Strauss, *Tristes Tropiques*, 1955.

At the end of the nineteenth century the plot of real estate on which this splendid building stands belonged to Count Sebastião Pinho, a Portuguese aristocrat who had settled in Rio de Janeiro. The private mansion on the property was demolished when it was purchased by the Guinle family. Today's palace was commissioned from the architects Joseph Gire (the Frenchman who also built the Copacabana Palace) and Armando da Silva Telles. The palace was erected between 1909 and 1914 as a home for the family of Eduardo junior, eldest son of Guilhermina and Eduardo Guinle's seven children.

The innovation at that time was that it was built in the center of the plot, the main front being preceded by a garden set as far back as feasible from the street. The asymmetric domes and slate roof are a clearly recognizable nod to the Renaissance influence of the châteaux of the Loire. The decor makes abundant recourse to noble materials: marble in various hues, granite, onyx, ebony, crystal, bronze, oak paneling, porcelain, and mirrors. Entering the palace, the refinement of the great hall on the ground floor is immediately irresistible. The flights of the majestic fan-shaped staircase with steps in Italian marble and bronze banisters diverge beneath a splendid example of French stained glass that lights the two landings.

Eduardo Guinle's fondness for the Casino at Monte-Carlo is betrayed not only on the façade but also within, where the decor in the mezzanine and the dining room is clearly inspired by the gaming emporium of the Principality of Monaco.

The French rocaille style prevails in the salons, illustrated by the silk and damask covering the chairs, the inlaid furniture, and ormolu ornaments. The master bathroom, featuring over three hundred square feet (thirty-one square meters) of Italian marble, crystal chandeliers, and English copper taps and fittings, is famous for being the largest and chicest in all Brazil. Built a few years later, the service wing derives more from the art nouveau style: a wall tapestry with flowers and birds and polychrome *azulejos* colored prior to glazing with a different pattern in the kitchen, the laundry, and the preserved baker's oven that is lined entirely with a relief wheatear motif.

Since 1975 this palace, which bears the name of the quarter in which it so gracefully stands, has been the official residence of the Governor of the State of Rio de Janeiro. ≈≈

FACING PAGE AND FOLLOWING DOUBLE PAGE Commissioned by the Guinle family from the architects Joseph Gire and Armando da Silva Telles, and built between 1909 and 1913, the palace today serves as the residence of the governor of the State of Rio de Janeiro. It is famous for being one of the most attractive and impressive buildings in the city.

The decor makes abundant recourse to
noble materials: marble in various hues, granite,
onyx, ebony, crystal, bronze, oak paneling,
porcelain, and mirrors.

ABOVE, FACING PAGE, AND FOLLOWING DOUBLE PAGE The interior decoration of the
palace borrows chiefly from the French styles of Louis XV and
Louis XVI. Among the many things to admire are paintings by Frans Post
and Taunay, a replica of Marie-Antoinette's piano when she was queen
of France, a mosaic in marble and ceramic gilded with 24-carat gold,
sculptures and French furniture with gilt-bronze dressings.

Built a few years later,
the service wing derives more
from the art nouveau style:
a wall tapestry with flowers and
birds and polychrome *azulejos*
colored prior to glazing.

PRECEDING DOUBLE PAGE AND ABOVE Built after the main body of the building,
the service wing is decorated in the art nouveau style.
FACING PAGE The frames around the mirrors in the bathroom
are made of Carrara marble, as are the basins and the large bathtub
carved with figures of children in *alto-* and *mezzo-rilievo*.

343

The asymmetric domes and slate roof are
a clearly recognizable nod to the Renaissance
influence of the châteaux of the Loire.

ABOVE AND FACING PAGE The garden hosts sculptures
by the Frenchman Émile Guillaume, a Medici vase with
a singularly beautiful low-relief in the classical style,
and an art nouveau vase in Carrara marble.

English Grandeur: the City Hall

"And on every square, on every hotel terrace, from every drawing-room window one has but to lift one's eyes to see all sorts of bizarre-looking peaks and horns shrouded in a somber coat of *floresta*: Tijuca, Gávea, Campo dos Antes, Corcovado, and the Profile of Louis XVI. Behind our back looms something immense, black, cooling, and shiny – and with one bound we can be in the midst of it." **Paul Claudel**, *L'Œil écoute*, 1946.

Built in the Georgian style between 1947 and 1950, located on Rua São Clemente in the Botafogo district, the Palácio da Cidade is Rio de Janeiro's City Hall. It initially housed the United Kingdom embassy and the ambassador's residence before being sold to the city in 1974, after all the embassies removed to the new capital, Brasília.

The charming elegance and harmony of the building emerge at the back of a vast garden encircled by marble sculptures. On the imposing frontage the pediment above the porch is borne on four columns; the majestic windows and suspended terraces provide glorious views over the garden. The order, proportions, and symmetry typical of the Georgian style are as enchanting inside as out. With green marble flooring and columns, the hall leads to staircases at the sides serving the floors above. The paintings too share the Georgian palette of pale green and beige. Framed by columns, the doors support pediments similar to that at the entrance, enriched by high-relief friezes of zoomorphic figures and acanthus leaves. The ceiling is decorated with polychrome rosettes. The conference room and its large oval table keep faith with the style of the palace, while the cornice and moldings on the ceiling echo motifs on the floor. The Brazilian furniture dates primarily from the eighteenth and nineteenth centuries.

The centrally placed garden floods the rooms with daylight and ensures a transition to all the other wings of the building. Contrasting with the classical decor of the rest of the edifice, a modern bronze sculpture by Agostinelli representing St. Sebastian, the patron saint of the city, stands tall among the plantations.

As an official building, the Palácio da Cidade is not open to the public, but events are held there and it may be possible to visit it by appointment. ≋

FACING PAGE Built in a neo-Georgian style between 1947 and 1950, the Palácio da Cidade used to serve as the Embassy of the United Kingdom and the residence of the ambassador, until all the embassies were transferred to Brasília. The City of Rio de Janeiro purchased it in 1974 and it is today the City Hall.

The order, proportions, and symmetry
typical of the Georgian style
are as enchanting inside as out.

FACING PAGE AND ABOVE The sober interior, the walls painted in pastel colors,
the doorframes with pediments and low-reliefs, and the ceiling adorned
with rosettes are typical of the Adam style fashionable in England
in the late eighteenth century.
FOLLOWING DOUBLE PAGE From the main gate one can admire the majestic
frontage of the building, with its terraces and four columns,
standing proudly at the rear of the immense garden.

Acknowledgments

Nicolas Martin Ferreira and the publisher would like to express their profound gratitude to all those who have collaborated in the publication of this book:

Sérgio Cabral, governor of the state of Rio de Janeiro, Eduardo Paes, mayor of Rio de Janeiro, Olavo Monteiro de Carvalho, Luciana and Ronaldo Cezar Coelho and Mara Fainziniber.

Special thanks to Lenny Niemeyer for her support and for giving permission to use bathing suit patterns from her collections.

They are very thankful to the House of Cartier, especially Christine Borgoltz and Michel Aliaga in Paris and Maxime Tarneaud in Brazil, for their support and enthusiasm.

For their time and generosity, they are especially thankful to: Fatima and Alvaro Otero, Monica and Paulo Jacobsen, Andrea and Guy Dellal, Andrea and Quinten Dreesmann, Hecilda and Sérgio Fadel, Jorge and Angelica Nobrega, Karen Couto, Sergio Parreiras, Emmanuelle and Philippe Meeus de Clermont Tonnerre, Genny and Selmo Nissenbaum, Mara and Marcio Fainziliber, João Niemeyer, Beatriz Millhazes, Tunga, Ricardo Nauenberg, Olivia Tarnowsky Fasanello, Ricardo Fasanello(†), Thiago Bernardes, Sergio Rodrigues, Claudia Fialho, Michael Roberts, Marcello and Mauricio Leite Barbosa, José Resende.

For their valuable assistance, special thanks to: the Marquês de Salamanca Institute, the São Fernando Institute, Fernando Chacel(†), Bernardo Jacobsen, Christiane Pasqualette, Iona Szkurnik do Rio, Claudia Gomes, Camilla Lacerda, Flavia Leal, Iomar de Camargo, Gisele Taranto, Libia Schenker, Maria Antonia Bocayuva, Sophie Bernard, Jackie and Maria Victoria de Botton, Tininha Falcao, Luciana Esteves, the staff of the fazendas Santarem, San Fernando and Chakrinha, the team of the hotel Insólito Boutique in Buzios, the Niemeyer Foundation, H. Stern Home, the House of Trousseau and the Copacabana Palace.

The photographer is particularly grateful to Tichotte and the Martin Ferreira family.